# Mama John

## The Lifelong Missionary
## Service of Mary Saunders

## Niña Ellison

New Hope
Birmingham, Alabama

New Hope
P. O. Box 12065
Birmingham, Alabama 35202-2065

Dewey Decimal Classification: B
                    922.6
Subject Headings: SAUNDERS, MARY
                  MISSIONARY BIOGRAPHY
                  MISSIONS, MEDICAL
                  MISSIONS—AFRICA

Scripture taken from the NEW AMERICAN STAN-
DARD BIBLE ®, © Copyright The Lockman
Foundation 1960, 1962, 1963, 1968, 1971, 1972, 1973,
1975, 1977. Used by permission.

Cover design by Barry Graham

ISBN: 1-56309-171-2
N964107•0596•7.5M1

# CONTENTS

# F O R E W O R D

Reading the manuscript of this book, I relived over 48 years of challenge. Life with Mama John has always been a surprise, or rather, an endless series of surprises. She has taken seriously the scriptural injunction of being a submissive wife; nevertheless, her commitment to being an obedient handmaiden of her Lord and Savior has always been a primary and absolute imperative in all the affairs of life. The role of husband and best friend has often created for me a searching of God's will in our lives.

This book can provide only a glimpse of a life lived in awareness of the presence and leading of God's Holy Spirit. Notes Mama John has jotted down in the margins of her tattered Bibles reveal communication from God through His Word which has prepared her for future events and critical decisions in her journey. Her prayer journals reveal the same phenomena.

Today, before I wrote this, we were discussing our last visit to the National Aeronautics and Space Administration (NASA), near Houston. While there, Mama John learned that plans are being considered to include senior adults in the space shuttle program in order to test the effects of weightlessness on the elderly. "Davis," she said, "When we travel to Houston in the fall, let's find out if I can apply. I'd love to do that, and I'm sure I can honor God in such an occasion."

Well, who knows? She's Mama John, and I am never surprised at the next challenge, whatever it is! My task is to care for her, support her, love her, and pray for her as God uses her committed life for His honor and glory.

Davis Saunders
March 1996

# MOGADISHU, SOMALIA

*"I have been anointed with fresh oil. The
righteous man will flourish like the palm tree,
He will grow like a cedar in Lebanon. Planted in
the house of the Lord, They will flourish in the
courts of our God. They will still yield fruit in old
age; They shall be full of sap and very green,
To declare that the Lord is upright; He is my rock,
and there is no unrighteousness in Him"*

*(Psalm 92:10b,12-15).*

**1992**

The sound of gunfire was deafening. Mama John, along with seven
other volunteers, moved to sit in the hallway. It seemed the safest
place to be as the fighting raged on around them.

"This is the UN task force commander. Stay where you are.
Remain low. Most of this is friendly fire." The voice crackled over
the shortwave radio that was transmitting to a handheld receiver.

"Friendly fire! It doesn't sound friendly to me," said a team
member.

"Those people yelling outside our gate don't sound friendly
either," responded another.

By the second day the hallway where the team of eight sat
seemed to shrink in size. An escape route had been planned and

now, unless their immediate safety was threatened, it was just a matter of sitting tight. There were 20 armed men within the compound—hired to protect the property. The UN helicopters on patrol were flying so close that the faces of the pilots could be seen. The noise was endless. Mortars, machine guns, and grenades boomed and crashed all around them. The smell of burning tires permeated the air, their smoke used to make effective roadblocks. Screams, chants, cries for help . . . the noise went on and on.

In her 70 years Mama John couldn't remember hearing such noise without relief. She sat quietly and read. *In a little while I'll go to the kitchen and get something to drink,* she thought.

"Would anyone like to help me make some grapefruit juice?" asked Martha Robison, volunteer nurse. "We were given a bushel of grapefruit at our last clinic!"

*Our last clinic* . . . Mama John remembered the clinic they had held two days before. She had anticipated being able to return the next day to a village not far from there; but then all this fighting had started and no one was going anywhere. In her mind she began planning for the next clinic. The boxes that held all of their supplies were packed and ready to go. The nurses normally did that in the evenings after holding clinic all day. The boxes would be loaded in a pickup truck along with the rickety folding chairs and tables that had been purchased at the local open-air market. They would meet at a prearranged place with the UN troops assigned to guard them. With a Humvee before them and one behind them, off they would go. Sometimes the UN troops were Americans, sometimes Nigerian, Italian, or Palestinian. It made for interesting conversations. After arriving at a village these trained troops would set up parameters and provide windows of safety so that the clinics could be held. During some of the more tense times, armed helicopters would circle above, attempting to guarantee a safe presence.

Mama John remembered the day when a team with an Irish nurse had been ambushed and killed. Mama John had been only a kilometer away at the time. . . .

She went to a village to try to help a dying man whose abdomen was swollen so large that he was unable to lie down, sit up, or stand. With his distended abdomen, the man's only goal was to breathe. His intense pain was obvious, though he never spoke a word.

On that day Mama John went with only two armed guards in a truck to take this man and his wife to the hospital in Mogadishu. Arriving at the hospital they pulled up next to a donkey pulling a wooden cart filled with sick people. The donkey was frail and pitiful but was nothing compared to those who sat waiting apathetically in the cart.

Once inside the hospital, Mama John found a physician's assistant who was willing to drain the excess fluid from the man's abdomen. It took a long time because there was so much fluid. Time had to be allowed in between the episodes of fluid removal for the abdomen to adjust. Finally the procedure was completed, and for the first time the man smiled.

"Thank you," he said in a quiet voice. His death was inevitable, but his pain level was more bearable. His eyes told that he knew this as well as Mama John did.

The man's wife had waited patiently, understanding little of what was happening, but willing to trust this white-haired woman. Mama John had motioned for her to come. They needed to buy food because the hospital did not provide such services. Together they went to a nearby stand where Mama John helped to purchase provisions.

When they returned to the hospital, they discovered that the man had been taken to the fourth floor where he had been given a space to place his mat and lie down.

The hospital full of patients had little else. There were no supplies or equipment, and very little staff. Because of the bombing, the walls were pockmarked and none of the windows remained intact. Jagged edges of glass could be seen hanging on to crumbling putty in blackened window frames. Holes gaped open where once there had been plumbing.

Mama John sighed. She knew there was no other choice. This was the best option for the man. As she left, he smiled again. Mama John knew she would be back to visit the next day.

It wasn't until she returned to the team house in the late afternoon that Mama John learned the fate of the young Irish nurse. Mama John and the other nurses stopped instantly and knelt to pray. Each recognized that it could have been one of them. Within their hearts they asked God to prepare them for whatever challenges lay ahead.

Mama John changed her position, leaning back against the wall of the hallway in the team house. She closed her eyes and began picturing the dusty road that led up to the village where they had held their last clinic.

After unloading their supplies under a single, lonely tree, they met with the village headman.

"You are welcome to our village," he said, smiling with a toothless grin.

"We have come because we want to help. Our God has asked us to help others who are in need," Mama John explained.

"You may speak to your God on our behalf," the headman responded.

Mama John couldn't believe her ears. This was the first time she had been invited to pray. Always before when she had mentioned God's role in her work the leaders had turned a deaf ear.

"May I speak so that the village can hear?" Mama John respectfully asked.

After a long pause, the village headman finally replied, "Let it be so."

So Mama John found herself in front of the village people.

"God, you are here today . . ." she began, pausing so that her interpreter could translate.

"We know Your love is a mighty thing and that You love every person here in this village. Help them to see Your love through the care that we nurses give today. Amen."

In the profound silence that followed, Mama John lifted her head. Her hair was covered with a scarf out of respect for the Muslim cultural requirements that a woman keep her head covered at all times while in public. Yet with her age and the love she showed, those who looked at Mama John in that moment sensed the presence of God.

The lines for treatment formed. Martha Robison handled immunizations and pediatrics, while Mama John and her daughter, Niña, also a nurse, saw the adults.

One 19-year-old girl came. She weighed no more than 50 pounds even though she was at least 5 feet 8 inches tall. Her father told how she refused to eat when food became scarce, sharing all she could find with her little brother. Mama John gave what she could in vitamins and high-protein biscuits to the girl, but she wondered if it was too late.

Another widow came with four children. All had ear infections, worms, and scabies (a contagious itch or mange with oozing crusts caused by parasitic mites). Their level of malnutrition was severe. Yet another came with a large wound on his arm that had gone untreated far too long. Another with a venereal disease . . . another with a urinary tract infection . . . another with pneumonia. At times the lines seemed endless.

The sun beat down mercilessly on them. Soon they would have to move their table to follow the sliver of shade that the withered tree provided.

*It is so hot*, Mama John thought as the sweat trickled down the small of her back. Her lips were dry and cracked. She could feel that her forehead was burned again. They had not had anything to drink. *How can we drink in front of these who have no water?* She decided to wait until the drive home.

She heard a crooning noise. Two little girls toddled toward her as fast as their frail legs would carry them. Their hair was burnt orange and their stomachs distended above sticklike legs. Yet their faces were aglow. They remembered this woman. She had helped them when they were so near death. The group she was with had brought food for the whole village for weeks. They reached Mama John and wrapped their tiny arms around her legs. Mama John stooped down to hug them. In her love she forgot the heat, the thirst, the fatigue. She remembered only that it was for such as these that she had come to Somalia.

Sitting in the hallway and waiting for rescue from the gunfire ringing all around them, Mama John found herself praying for the patients she had cared for. She thought back to her first patient.

He was an older man with a terrible sore on his leg. Mama John showed him how to clean and dress the wound. She then gave him a course of antibiotics to take and planned when she would see him again.

He brought his wife to meet her one day. She, too, was elderly, her face a study in wrinkles. As she smiled it was easy to see that most of her teeth were missing. She wore a homespun cotton dress that had seen much use. In the style of the women here, her head was covered with a loose weave cotton cloth. The color of her head cloth was the same earth tone as her dress.

She invited Mama John to visit their home on her next clinic day.

The following week, remembering her invitation, she went to the edge of the village where there was a moundlike structure of woven branches and reeds much like all the others in the village. As Mama John entered through the small opening, she noticed that there was not one piece of furniture or decoration. The floor, where she was invited to sit, was packed hard from the many footfalls over time.

To her left was a hole where the wall had caved in. Mama John saw that the older woman was busy patching the opening with a combination of mud and cow dung that was mixed together in the container sitting beside the wall. The mixture was adhering to the wattle, and after drying, would be polished. Mama John knew it was the cow dung that gave the wall its shine.

Realizing she had a visitor, the woman's face broke out in a smile. She immediately wiped off her hands and greeted Mama John.

They smiled at each other. Neither knew the other's language.

A young interpreter appeared, and the woman spoke.

"She says her grandchildren are ill," the young girl interpreted.

"Tell her to bring them to the clinic area. I will see if I can help them," Mama John replied.

Smiles again.

Mama John stood up to go; but the woman put a restraining arm on her shoulder, spoke rapidly in Amharic, and then left.

"Wait," the interpreter said.

A few minutes later the woman reappeared. In her hand were two small brown eggs. A gift—a treasure to both the giver and the receiver.

Mama John continued her hallway prayer, "Lord, thank you for these . . ."

"So would you like some grapefruit juice?" Martha asked again.

Mama John came out of her reverie and accepted a glass of fresh-squeezed, room temperature, grapefruit juice.

The deafening noise continued—no point trying to converse. To speak you had to shout straight into the ears of the person you wished to speak with.

Mama John closed her eyes again. She was supposed to return to the US at the end of the week. Months of caring for the sick and hungry in Somalia and now her term of volunteer service was over. Yet strangely, leaving now seemed impossible. She prepared herself for a delay.

Mama John began reading her Bible. She needed to prepare for the evening hour when she and a young Somali would meet to study the Bible together. They met each evening in secret. Mama John knew Christianity was forbidden by those who adhered to the government-approved Islamic faith. The few who chose to follow Christ did so in secret or faced the death threats placed on their lives. These evening meetings had been the highlight of Mama John's assignment. She recalled the previous evening.

"Let's say the verse together that we have been learning," Mama John encouraged.

"This is the day the Lord has made . . ." they began together.

When they finished the verse Mama John sang the familiar chorus based on the passage.

"This is great," said the young Christian. "When there is more than one Christian, what other things do you do?"

Mama John realized that the ideas of group worship, music, choirs, and all those other aspects that she took for granted, were unimaginable to this one who had only known reading the Bible and praying in secret solitude. She was silent for a moment, and then she reached over and wrapped her arms around the precious young person.

"God," she began to pray, "bless this one who seeks to know You. Thank You that You can be found in the very corners of this earth. Help us to continue to seek You more."

"Did you know," Mama John asked her companion after their prayer, "that I have had a dream?"

"A dream?" he asked.

"Yes," Mama John replied.

"Tell me . . ." he said.

"In my dream I see the city of Mogadishu," Mama John began. "In the middle of that city is a strong, evangelical church. I see a place where Somalis can go, if they choose, to discover Christ. In my dream we are free to worship as we desire."

Silence.

"It is a powerful dream," said the young Somali thoughtfully.

Mama John sat in the hallway and continued her review of the past few months. The country she was in was known as the "Horn of Africa." It was a v-shaped land with a population of almost 10 million. The tall, slender, and light brown Somali people had previously been more united than many other African groups. They had a common language, Somali; a common religion, Islam; and a common set of traditions. Yet, in spite of this cultural unity, Mama John saw deep divisions: differences in clans and differences in social order for members within each clan. A caste system divided people into "high caste" or "low caste." The lines were nonnegotiable.

Mogadishu, once a thriving seaport and capital city, was a hollow shell with its infrastructure destroyed. The beautiful buildings and hotels were now barren reminders of what man's destructive power can do. Wires hung limply from poles. None of the normal systems functioned—no water, communications, or trash removal—just a million people trying to survive a civil war with no end in sight.

A line divided the city into north and south. Warring clans occupied each side. This line, called the "green line," was now heavily guarded by UN troops trying to restore peace between the warring Somalis. The two sides of the city functioned separately, even down to having a separate currency. To travel from one side to the other, different vehicles had to be obtained, for "north" cars would be shot at in the "south" area. The team Mama John was working with had set up feeding stations or clinics on both sides of the city.

Three of the feeding stations were centered in inner-city camps that had sprung up as the many displaced people settled there. The "houses" were made of plastic, cardboard, and sticks. Hundreds of people lived there, mostly women and children who had fled their homes because of the war. Three times a day hired women cooked a high-protein mixture for the children to eat. The cooking containers were large enough to feed hundreds of people. The ingredients were mixed with large wooden paddles and cooked over an open fire. The women had found that the best pot stabilizers were empty mortar shells placed in triangular fashion in the fire.

The needs in these camps were overwhelming. Mama John

remembered how happy she had been with the arrival of the well-staffed, well-stocked team called Samaritan's Purse, who willingly stepped in to lead the medical relief efforts of these camps.

"Lunch is ready," called one of the team members to those sitting in the hallway. A lull prevailed in the noise from outside.

*Has everyone stopped for lunch?* she wondered.

The others moved to the dining room, but Mama John stayed back, remembering one of her first lunches in Mogadishu.

A young woman had been hired to cook for them and to have a meal ready when they came in from the clinics. It had sounded like a great idea. The woman had produced references from a European family she worked for prior to the war.

The first day, the cook had prepared a fried meat patty, collard greens mixed with scrambled eggs, a tossed salad, and rice. Mama John took a bite of the meat.

She could hear her jaws working up and down, up and down. The meat seemed like a sponge that grew as it gained moisture and momentum.

"What kind of meat is this?" she asked.

"Camel," the cook replied.

"Camel!" Mama John choked out. No wonder it was so tough and resilient, defying being chewed and swallowed in a normal manner, soaking in moisture at every point. She thought of the light-brown camels she had seen going to the market that morning. They had looked like "real survivors" straight from the desert!

*Oh well*, she thought, *there's still the salad.*

All of the team members enjoyed the salad. In fact, it was the only thing finished when the meal was over.

Within the hour, however, they all had a problem. Diarrhea had hit and hit hard. With only two bathrooms in the house, lines of squirming volunteers formed.

"How did you clean the salad before you served it?" they asked.

"Clean? It was clean. I buy it clean from the market," the cook responded defensively. It was obvious that she didn't like her kitchen techniques questioned.

The next day no one was quite ready for another helping of the salad the cook prepared; and Mama John still couldn't stomach the camel meat that was served.

Then one day the UN came to their rescue by offering some of their MREs (meals ready to eat). From then on, setting the table consisted of putting a small pair of scissors or a sharp knife at everyone's place so that the tough plastic containers holding the ready-made food could be opened.

Mama John stood up, stretched, and left the hallway to move to the dining area and pick out her black plastic packets.

"Let's see, do I want macaroni and cheese, au gratin potatoes, ham, or chicken and dumplings? What have the rest of you picked?" she asked.

The routine was for each team member to pick something different so that the various meals could be passed around and shared. It was like gleaning from a smorgasbord, of sorts.

Lunch over, the team returned to the hallway. Things still seemed quieter. *Perhaps my departure will not be delayed after all,* thought Mama John.

The next morning the team's financial coordinator came in from communicating with the UN task force.

"They have found a way out of Somalia for you and Niña. If you do not go now it may be days before there is another opening."

Several days earlier they had lost radio contact with their team headquarters in a neighboring country. With the escalated fighting Mama John knew her family would be concerned. They did not know how she had fared during these last few days of "hallway living."

Within minutes Mama John and Niña were packed and ready to go. The driver sped through the streets of Mogadishu to the airport. UN troops lined the streets. The roadside was pockmarked with oblong irregularities in the barren soil of the roadside— unmarked graves of those who had died during recent civil clashes.

They had been buried with haste in the dark of the night by others who feared for their own safety. The armed guards in the vehicle kept their guns at a ready angle.

At the airport, Mama John and Niña were greeted by an Australian soldier and told where to wait. The ramshackle terminal showed the effects of countless bombings. Its tin roof drooped without benefit of support. On the runway, troops repaired holes in the tarmac. The noises of war reverberated throughout the city.

*Could we really be leaving?* Mama John wondered.

Mama John and Niña said good-bye to those who had brought them. The young Somali Christian was at Mama John's side. They bid each other farewell. As they leaned toward each other for a final hug, Mama John heard these words whispered in her ear, "Keep dreaming your dreams, mother, and together may we dream that I might be the pastor of that first church here in this city."

Through the tears of a joyful heart, Mama John turned to see the Australian trooper in front of them.

"The plane has made it," he said. "I'll warn you mates, it's an old Russian cargo plane. You'll be sitting on metal jump seats that fold down from the sides of the plane. It's not the latest in comfort."

They walked across the sizzling pavement. Heat waves danced around their legs as they made their way to the rear of the aircraft where a large entryway folded down from the belly of this huge, man-made bird. A crewman motioned for them to enter. It was clear that he spoke no English; neither did the pilot. The plane was not fitted with the common amenities of commercial airlines—no intercom, no takeoff announcement, no flight attendant, no bathroom.

Taking off, the heavy plane banked sharply to the left to avoid the city of Mogadishu and the possibility of being a target for gunfire. Mama John found she was looking directly down on the destroyed city of Mogadishu for the last time. She closed her eyes to rest.

Niña leaned over and asked, "Are you OK?"

"Yes, I'm fine . . . just a little tired," Mama John responded. She was bone tired. This had not been an easy assignment.

Eyes closed, she thought back to the first time, months before, when the Lord had placed a burden on her heart for Somalia. In her prayertime she had committed to preparing herself. During that time, she wrote in a letter to her daughter:

*I know that I don't understand just what God wants me to do, but I have sensed such an overwhelming burden for Somalia. I know He is preparing me for something. I find myself praying for those in Somalia throughout each day. As time goes by I will discover my role in this.*

At 70, Mama John was ready for service and to do whatever God asked of her.

With this preparation, it had been no surprise when a call came through from the director of a relief program for Somalia. Would she initiate and lead the medical effort for a team going into Somalia? Even though there had been no prior communication Mama John had been expecting such a call. Why else would God have placed such a heavy burden on her heart for the Somalis?

"I have been ready and waiting," had been her response.

Within two weeks she was on a flight to Africa. She was confident, not in her own abilities, but in the ability of her heavenly Father to lead her in the paths that she should follow. In these past months as she had read and reread Psalm 92, she had known that she was anointed with a fresh oil, and challenged to flourish. She knew that it had been a part of God's plan for her to come and help in Somalia.

She remembered the questions she had been asked as she packed in preparation for her assignment.

"Mama John, why would you become involved in a crisis of such proportions?"

"How can a woman of 70 face such difficulties, such hardships?"

"How will you know what to do once you get to this country that seems bent on self-destruction?"

To understand the answer to these questions and more, come and catch a glimpse of the journey of one incredible woman, Mama John.

# CHAPTER 2

# CHARLESTON,
# SOUTH CAROLINA

*"For God so loved the world, that He gave His only
begotten Son, that whoever believes in Him should not
perish, but have eternal life"*

*(John 3:16).*

Mary Pauline Hogg was born in Charleston, South Carolina, on August 10, 1923, the only girl in a family with five sons. However, our story really begins when Mary was 13 years old, for it was then that she made the decision to believe that Jesus Christ was the Lord and Savior of her life. Although her family did not attend church, Mary, in her own heart, sensed an inner spiritual need. At an early age she began attending Sunday School and church faithfully at Citadel Square Baptist Church on Meeting Street in Charleston.

It was at Citadel Square Baptist Church that her life was touched by a woman named Duna Caldwell. Duna taught Mary's Sunday School class. Duna became her friend and cared for her in a special way. Duna sometimes stopped by Mary's home to walk with her to church.

One day as they walked, Duna asked Mary, "What are you going to do when you grow up?"

"I would like to be a nurse," Mary responded. Secretly she dreamed of one day being able to care for Duna so that in some small way she could repay her kindness.

The love and caring of Duna brought Mary to a beginning understanding of God's love. One Sunday, at the end of the morning worship service, she walked forward to publicly tell of the faith she had discovered.

At the age of 14, Mary went to work at Kress's Department Store. She worked after school and on Saturdays, which were especially long because her regular hours were from 10:30 A.M. to 10:30 P.M. Still, Mary gladly took opportunities to work even longer because with the overtime her salary increased from $1.63 to $1.83 for the day.

Mary made college a priority at an early age; however, college was not a part of her parent's plans for her. Her conversation with them confirmed their differences.

"Mary, your mother and I both work for the railroad. It's a good job."

"Yes, Dad, but I would like to go to college to become a nurse."

"That'll take a lot of time and money—money we don't have. Why, I can help you get a good job at the railroad as soon as you graduate from high school, and you'll be set for the rest of your life. You can be settled and secure with a good salary."

"I'm sorry, Mom and Dad, but I'm just not sure that is what life has in store for me," Mary responded with sadness and determination at the same time. She felt badly for not going along with her parents' plans.

There was a heavy silence. Then, her dad sighed as he stood up to leave.

"All right, but if you go on to school, you'll have to pay your own way," he said.

So Mary worked long hours at every opportunity and saved every penny she earned. After high school she went to work full time at Kress's. After a year, however, she had to accept that college was an impossibility for her financially. Still, she pursued her dream of becoming a nurse with determination and entered the nursing school at Roper Hospital in Charleston.

Nurse training was demanding with the students often working 12-hour shifts in the hospital in addition to class work and homework. Mary had the usual anxiety of a student nurse the first time she entered a patient's room to help with a bed bath.

"Good morning," she said brightly, hoping that the cheerful sound of her voice would cover up her nervousness.

The elderly man just nodded.

"I'll help you with your bath," explained Mary as she reached for the bath blanket and began covering her patient just as she had been taught—first one side, then the other, top to bottom. She patted the bed. Where was his second leg? Pat, pat, pat. She looked up to see a pair of eyes watching her movements with interest.

"Comfortable?" she asked, more to pass the awkward moment than for concern of his well-being.

"Whacha doin?" the man asked.

"Oh," she tried to say nonchalantly, "this is how we are taught to give a bath."

"Seems like a lot of pat-patting to me. Where's the soap and water?"

"Coming right up." Embarrassed, but determined, Mary stopped her patting and began to bathe him. She remembered then that the man had only one leg; the other had been amputated. In her nervousness she had forgotten! For the first time, but not the last, things did not go "by the book" for student nurse Hogg.

In her senior year, life changed drastically. With the bombing of Pearl Harbor, the United States entered into the Second World War. A shortage of nurses brought about the start of a senior cadet program, and Mary became a cadet.

1944: Mary's graduation picture from the Medical University of South Carolina.

One of her assignments that year was the emergency room. One night a Chinese man was brought in by his son. While the father was being treated, Mary went to speak to the son sitting in the waiting room.

"You are waiting for your father?"

Mary asked the obvious, trying to start a conversation.

"Yes, how is he?" the young man responded.

"He is doing much better. How are you doing?"

Mary learned that this young man's name was Robbie. For the first time in her life she sensed the Holy Spirit leading her to ask Robbie about his own spiritual walk.

"I'll pray for your father, and I'll pray for you," she said. "Would that be OK?"

"Oh, yes. I would like to know more about praying. Are you a Christian?"

Mary couldn't believe her ears. He was so eager to learn. She invited him to church and to meet her pastor.

In the weeks to follow, Robbie went to church with Mary, and after some time, he became a Christian. Mary knew she would never forget that first time when God allowed her to be a part of leading someone to know Christ Jesus; and yet, at the time, she was unaware of the many ways that Robbie's life would continue to affect the Kingdom of God. Years later, as a furloughing missionary, Mary was introduced by Robbie before speaking at a large, inner-city church. He had become a leader within the Christian family.

Following nursing school, Mary got a job as night nursing supervisor. She worked 7:00 P.M. to 7:00 A.M. five nights a week, and then 7:00 P.M. to 12:00 A.M. the sixth night. The hospital was short staffed, so Mary stayed busy.

She was not too busy, however, to begin to make long-awaited wedding plans. She had been engaged to Bill Taylor since high school. They had dated for five years, and now the wedding plans were underway.

Bill was away on duty as a merchant seaman, but they looked forward to marrying when he returned home on leave.

Yet, Mary's plans changed once again. The need for army nurses was increasing; Mary had three brothers that were already involved in the war effort. She heard constant reports of the need for nurses and realized that she could no longer stay uninvolved. So, while Bill was still away and against his wishes, Mary decided to join the army. As a single nurse with no responsibilities at home, she felt the need to do her part for her country.

Army life at Camp Gordon in Augusta, Georgia, brought many changes in Mary's life. One change came following her first gas-mask drill. Mary lined up with the new

1945: Mary and a friend walk to work at Roper Hospital in Charleston, South Carolina.

recruits as the procedure was explained and gas masks were handed out. She understood she would need to move quickly to put the mask on.

*Ow*, she thought as she rolled the strap over her head. She discovered to her dismay that her bun was a tangled web woven about the strap. Struggling, she looked up into the eyes of her leader; there was no sign of humor.

"Lieutenant Hogg, you would have died three times if this had been a real emergency. GI haircut is ordered before 0600 tomorrow."

Later that day Mary watched her thick masses of auburn hair fall to the floor. She hadn't realized how much her hair meant to her. Discouraged, Mary headed back to her barracks; but someone stopped her to say she had a phone call.

"Mary?" Her mother's familiar voice was a welcome sound.

"Mom, how are you? Is everything OK?"

"I have some bad news for you. It's about Bill."

*No*, thought Mary, *surely Bill has not been hurt or killed*. She had just sent him a long letter discussing many of their wedding plans.

"Bill has come home, Mary, but he married someone that he met while he was on shore leave. I'm sorry, sweetie. I know this is no way to find out."

Mary spoke to her mother for a few minutes, hung up the phone, and slowly walked away. She felt herself pulling off her engagement ring, and the tears began to flow. Mary's heart ached with the pain, but she knew what she had to do. Through her tears she found an envelope, addressed it to Bill, and put the ring inside.

Camp Gordon was a training ground. One way the army prepared soldiers for what they would find was to create a small Japanese village on the base, and run them through mock skirmishes and drills. Live ammunition was used.

One day while Mary was on duty, an injured soldier was brought in. His eyes were roughly bandaged and his face was bloody and burned. A hand grenade had exploded prematurely during a drill. This young, handsome soldier named Ralph would no longer be going to war. His eyesight was gone.

As Mary cared for him, she grieved. He would need to relearn how to live again. His mother came and Mary met her.

"I have been so worried about him going overseas, so fearful that he would be injured or die. But I never dreamed that this would happen before he even began. I feel so sick inside," Ralph's mother confided in Mary through her tears. Mary tried to comfort her, but she felt so inadequate.

Life as an army nurse was not easy, and Mary struggled in many ways. She was lonely and realized that she was surrounded by soldiers looking for a date.

And so she began to date, dating men she would not have ordinarily dated, going to places she would not have gone. She tried to bury her loneliness in parties and dancing. But, as much as she loved to dance, her loneliness persisted.

She began to realize that she was headed off track. On New Year's Eve, she went to one of the wildest parties she had ever attended.

*What am I doing here?* she asked herself.

In times past, she had always spent New Year's Eve at church. Those were times of fun and fellowship, with the first minutes of the new year spent in a commitment of service to God.

*Oh God*, she prayed, *forgive me, cleanse me, and help me to recommit myself to You. I have been trying to plan my own life, and I am failing.*

Mary continued in the routine of army life until she received another message from home. Her mother was critically ill and needed her help. Mary requested and was granted an honorable discharge. She returned home.

Back home Mary learned that not only was her mother ill, but also her beloved Duna, her mentor. Mary went often to the hospital to care for Duna.

One day Duna reached out and grabbed Mary's hand, holding it in her own. She smiled at the young woman she had led to Christ.

*Duna is so very weak,* thought Mary. *Could this be our last time together?*

Duna spoke quietly with Mary, sharing fond memories. Then she asked, "Mary, will you come again tomorrow and fix my hair? I love it when you do it for me."

Mary smiled gently and responded, "Of course I'll come."

"Sit on the bed by me, Mary."

Again Duna reached out and held Mary's hand.

"The Lord is my shepherd, I shall not want. . . . I know whom I have believed and I am convinced that He is able to guard what I have entrusted to Him until that day" (Psalm 23:1; 2 Tim. 1:12b).

As Duna spoke these familiar words her hand fell from Mary's and her tired eyes closed as if she could hold them open no longer.

Later that evening Duna Caldwell died. It was with great difficulty that Mary went to the funeral home the next day and received permission to fulfill her promise. Quietly and lovingly she fixed the hair of the woman who had introduced her to the real meaning of life.

Mary once again began attending Citadel Square Baptist Church each week. God had worked in Mary's life through her experiences in the army, and it was at this time that she announced to the church that she felt called to go to Africa as a missionary nurse. Her acceptance into New Orleans Baptist Seminary set her direction and, once again, she was excited about the future.

In the meantime, Citadel Square Baptist Church continued to be her home. She taught youth Sunday School and worked with the young people on Sunday evenings. One of her friends at that time was Elwyn Saunders.

One Sunday evening as she and Elwyn walked into church together, he suggested that they sit with his older brother. Sitting by himself was Davis Saunders, a recently discharged marine lieutenant.

*Sure,* thought Mary, *I'd be more than happy to go sit by that good-looking young man. Hmmm.*

The next Wednesday evening Mary saw Davis as she walked to the midweek prayer service.

"Hello, Mary," Davis greeted her. "I've just brought my mother to the prayer service, and I have to pick her up in about an hour-and-a-half. Would you like to go out and get something to eat while I wait?"

"Thanks, I would like to but . . . ," Mary hesitated, "actually I was on the way to the prayer service myself."

They said good-bye.

On her way into church Mary stopped to talk with some friends. By the time she entered the room, to her surprise, there sat Davis. She smiled and joined him.

They began to date soon after that evening. A serious relationship developed rapidly, causing Mary some problems as she thought about her calling.

One evening she prayed, "Lord, You know that I am beginning to love Davis an awful lot. But I committed to You when I sensed You calling me to go to the missions

1946: Davis and Mary during their courtship.

field as a nurse. Father, I am willing to go, but what should I do about Davis? I ask that You give me an inner peace about my relationship with him."

Davis was an engineering student at the Citadel, a military college in South Carolina. He was finishing his degree, and he did not feel a call of any sort to missions work.

The next evening Davis and Mary sat by Colonial Lake. It was beautiful and serene, but sensing that their relationship was at a point where decisions would need to be made, Mary felt such inner turmoil.

They discussed the situation. On the one hand, Mary felt such a definite call to foreign missions, and on the other, she also felt a strong desire to be Davis's wife.

"Mary," Davis finally said, "I love God and I want to serve Him, but I can't say what I am going to do. I am studying to be an engineer and that's not exactly what you think of when you think of missions material."

Mary sat silently. She didn't have an answer. As the evening ended, the issue remained unresolved.

The next week Mary sought the advice of a trusted friend, Miss Olive Allen, education director of Citadel Square Baptist Church. Mary poured out her heart to Miss Allen.

"Miss Allen," she concluded, "I know I love Davis and he loves me, and we both love and want to serve God. Why do our paths seem to be heading in such different directions?"

"Mary, we do not always have the answers for our future plans, but we can ask for peace as we try to follow God in the present."

"I'm not sure what you mean," Mary said.

"It seems to me that you are trying to solve your whole life's plan at one time. Perhaps you should just look at the first step—Davis. I will tell you this, I cannot believe that you will go to the missions field as a single nurse. If you go to seminary you will probably get married," Miss Allen explained.

"But . . ." Mary tried to interrupt.

"Just wait, let me finish." Miss Allen continued, "Davis is an exceptional young man and I believe God is going to use his life in a wonderful way. If you have a peace about marrying him, marry him. Young men like him are not that easy to find. I know that Davis, too, wants to follow God. If you try to follow God together, He has promised that He will be found by those who seek Him."

This answer was what Mary had been searching for. Even though she did not understand the answer to her

1947: Davis and Mary on their wedding day.

own call to missions, she felt a peace about her decision. On September 14, 1947, Mary Pauline Hogg became Mrs. Davis Saunders following the Sunday morning worship service at Citadel Square Baptist Church.

The young couple honeymooned at Myrtle Beach, South Carolina, a location known for its sunshine and beautiful beaches. However, as they arrived so did the rain.

As they got out of the car Mary went to help unpack.

"Davis," she teased, "what did you put in this suitcase? I can't lift it."

She noticed he had brought two bags and she had only one.

As they settled down in the room, she saw to her surprise that the second heavy suitcase had books in it! However as it continued to rain, the young bride, at first disconcerted to be accompanied by a suitcase full of books, sat down and found herself reading alongside her new husband.

This was not the only unplanned aspect of Mary's honeymoon,

for the next day she received a phone call that her mother was once again critically ill. The honeymoon was cut short—rain, books, and all.

As newlyweds, Mary continued her nursing job and Davis resumed his studies in civil engineering. They didn't have much money, but it was a happy time.

Neither could cook so they bought a cookbook. Their meal combinations were often failures, but together they learned. When the food was too bad, they went down to the corner drugstore and Davis treated Mary to an Eskimo Pie. The simplicity of those days belied the changes that were to come.

The first of many changes came three months later on a Sunday morning. As they were singing the final hymn in the evening worship service, Davis left Mary's side to walk to the front of the church.

Mary's heart began to beat faster; this was so out of character for Davis.

Davis cleared his throat and began, "I have something I want to share with you this evening. I know this will come as a surprise to many of you, including my wife."

Mary nodded her head and smiled to encourage him. She felt a lump starting to build in her throat.

*What is he saying?* she wondered.

"For the past few months I have been sensing a new direction in my life. I believe God is calling me to work full time in Christian ministry. I am asking for your support and encouragement. Uh, that's all I have to say."

Mary felt the tears in her eyes. Davis had not spoken with her about this new direction in his life. She sensed that he had been waiting for an assurance that this new direction was from God.

In the months to follow Davis completed his degree in engineering. Then, with their eyes on their heavenly Father, the young couple turned their steps toward Southern Baptist Theological Seminary in Louisville, Kentucky.

CHAPTER 3

# LOUISVILLE, KENTUCKY

*"Now the Lord said to Abram, 'Go forth from*
*your country, And from your relatives*
*And from your father's house,*
*To the land which I will show you'"*

*(Gen. 12:1).*

Tickets in hand, Mary and Davis boarded a train in September 1947 that would take them away from family, friends, and all things familiar. The trip that began with breakfast in South Carolina lasted throughout the day and night. Early the next morning, their old friends from home, Chester and Lib Russell, met them at the Louisville train station.

Upon arriving in Louisville, they made their way to the Southern Baptist Theological Seminary campus. They registered and then found their lodgings on campus—room 247 in Manley Hall. Their new home was one room with a closet. Living in 247 on the second floor was more convenient for Mary than for Davis, because the women's bathroom was on this floor. The men's bathroom was on the third floor.

Their first free morning Davis and Mary took the city bus to downtown Louisville where they purchased the things they needed for housekeeping. Their furniture consisted of a bed, a foldout table with drawers, and paper drapes bought from Sears and Roebuck for $1.

As students, their budget was tight. Their total income each month was from the GI Bill: $102 for Davis and $75 for Mary. They ate in the seminary cafeteria only when they could afford it. On weekends they used the Russells' kitchenette, who went out of town to the church where he was pastor. Usually they prepared dried beans and rice, making enough for several meals. On special occasions they bought three chicken backs for 10 cents and boiled them with the rice. Having these precooked meals in their room during the week helped them survive on a meager income.

One morning, Davis surprised Mary.

"Breakfast is served," he proudly announced. "Toast and coffee for my favorite wife."

"Toast?" asked Mary. "How did you make us toast?"

"It's the newest thing, the latest invention. It's called the iron-toaster."

The only heating element they owned was an electric iron. Davis showed Mary how he had rigged a small wooden board with two levels of screws. Placed on the first level, the iron toasted one piece of bread. At the second level, it toasted a whole sandwich.

During the first year both Mary and Davis attended classes. But by the second year of seminary, it became evident that one of them would have to go to work full time. So, Mary took a job as seminary nurse and continued to audit classes.

Living conditions improved for them that year because of Mary's job on campus. They moved from Manley Hall to the infirmary apartment, and part of Mary's salary was a meal pass for the two of them to the cafeteria. The iron was retired to its original use.

One afternoon Mary returned home from having an eye exam to find a message that the seminary nurse was needed on the football field. The eye drops used for her eye exam had dilated her pupils and her vision was blurred.

The intramural finals, the Josephus Bowl, were in progress. One of the final teams was the South Carolina team for which Davis played.

Mary arrived at the sidelines to help the student who had been hurt. The skin above his eye was badly cut and blood flowed freely. Mary leaned closer to see better and then in a startled voice said, "Davis?"

"Didn't you know it was me?" he asked.

"I can't see too well right now," she confessed.

Helping each other, they walked back to the clinic where Mary did her best to clean the wound. That done, she helped take him to the doctor for the stitches that were needed.

"Preach on, brother."

"Amen."

"Say it again."

"That's right."

Davis paused in his message to look out at the congregation. Once a month during their first year at seminary, he and Mary attended a church of American Baptists. How Mary loved the music and informal worship! On these Sunday mornings they took the bus to downtown Louisville for worship. They always felt welcome though they did not easily blend in with the crowd.

And now he had been asked to preach.

"You don't preach too bad for a white man," Davis was told later. "You come back now."

And so they did. And Davis preached again. Each time Davis preached, the members took up a love offering for Davis and Mary. It was always more than enough to cover their bus fare.

Downtown on Sunday brought another treat for Mary. Davis usually took her to eat at the Blue Boar Restaurant for lunch, known for its good food and great prices.

Because of this preaching experience, Davis was asked to serve at Freedonia Baptist Church on Tapps Ridge outside of Vevay, Indiana.

He arrived home after his first visit.

"Tell me about the church," Mary asked.

"There are 15 members. It's an old church built with flat stones laid fitted tightly together with no mortar used—and there is a small outhouse out back," Davis said with a grin.

"Were the members glad to see you?"

"Well, one of the first members I spoke with was the chairman of the deacons. He told me that he was really from the Church of Christ but that he attended the Baptist church because it was closer."

"What did you say?" Mary asked.

"I didn't say anything, I just listened," Davis replied.

"Did they ask us to come?"

"Yes, they want us to come every other week to help lead the services. They clearly outlined our job. When we arrive for the morning worship service, we are to sweep out the church and light a fire in the potbellied stove, if needed. You need to help with the singing and I'll preach."

"Did they talk about a salary?"

"We will be given $15 each week that we come."

It wasn't much; nevertheless this was a time of learning and growing.

God blessed their time at the church. Before they left, Freedonia Baptist Church doubled in size to 30, and Davis baptized 12 new Christians.

"Betty has been here," Mary commented as they walked into their apartment one day after classes.

"I noticed the shavings, too," Davis said.

Lavelle and Betty Seats were missionaries from Nigeria. Lavelle was visiting professor of missions on campus, so Betty often came by to visit—bringing her pet parrot. If she had errands to run, Betty left the bird on the arm of one of Davis and Mary's chairs. The bird always sharpened his beak on the cheap wooden chair. So, Davis and Mary would know who their visitor had been by the wood shavings on the floor.

On one occasion, Mary told Davis as he came in from classes, "I think Betty has been here this morning."

"Did you see her?" Davis inquired.

"No."

"I don't see any shavings. Did she leave a message?"

"Sort of. Go look in the bathroom," Mary responded, the laughter in her eyes and the hint of a smile betraying the humor in the situation.

Davis poked his head around the bathroom door to see a duck swimming in the bathtub!

Yet, the Seats introduced them to more than just unusual pets; they introduced them to ideas about ministering in Africa and the tremendous needs there.

That year, George Sadler conducted student interviews for the Foreign Mission Board on the Southern campus. Davis was convinced that God was leading them to Africa because of his experiences in classes and seminary chapel services, and through his relationships with other Christians. Quietly he prayed, asking God for direction in his and Mary's lives. Finally, he made an appointment to meet with George Sadler.

After talking with George, Davis returned home.

"Mary, I've got something important to tell you," began Davis. "I've just been meeting with someone from the Foreign Mission Board."

Mary wondered, *Could it be that the Lord is leading Davis into missions?* She could barely contain her excitement.

"I met with George Sadler because I believe God wants us to be willing to go into missions work. We spoke about the possibility of going to Africa."

Mary remembered the hours they had spent agonizing over the decision of their marriage because of this very issue. She had known that it was the right thing to marry Davis and she had gained a God-given peace even though she didn't have the answer to her own commitment to missions. Now, in God's timing, she was beginning to understand. God was wanting her to follow Him step by step.

Their third and final year of seminary, Davis and Mary began to set their sights on Africa. Yet, they were aware that these years allowed them to make special friendships—lifetime friendships. Throughout their seminary years they were members of Walnut Street Baptist Church, even when serving in other churches part time. The pastor, William Pettigrew, who had also been their pastor at Citadel Square Baptist Church in South Carolina and had baptized both of them, was the first to know of their decision to go overseas. They had also found friends such as Clyde and Ann Enzor, Betty and Paul Jeans, Wicky and Bill Lawrence, Una Mae and Arthur Christmas, Walt and Bea Luckett, and Helen Coleman—friends who would serve as their support system and uphold them with love and prayers in the years to come.

On January 16, 1951, baby Mary Lee Saunders arrived. Mary had a normal delivery, but she suffered with a kidney infection afterward and remained in the hospital for ten additional days. Her recovery was an answer to the prayers offered for her during a special service held on the seminary campus.

The day she and Lee left the hospital, Mary's mother was there to help. They bathed Lee and put her to bed; but, later that evening, Mary's mother found Mary walking around in a daze.

"It's 2:00 A.M., Mary. What are you doing up?" she asked.

"The baby hasn't woken up yet," Mary responded.

"Did you check on her?"

"Yes, she's sleeping fine."

"Then why are you awake?" her mother asked, still perplexed.

"Because babies are supposed to wake up during the night. Everyone knows that. I think I'll wake her up and feed her and then go back to bed," the obviously worried Mary said.

And so the little baby was woken up, fed, and tucked back into bed.

"You need to leave that baby alone and let her sleep," advised Mary's mother.

From that night on, Lee slept through the night, and the new mother, Mary, learned not to wake her up!

As the time for graduation drew near, Davis and Mary were invited to travel to Richmond, Virginia, by train to be appointed as foreign missionaries and to learn more about their assignment. George Sadler asked them if they would consider starting new work in the Gold Coast (now Ghana). They said they were willing, but after arriving in Richmond, they learned that they were being sent to Nigeria, the only country in Africa where Southern Baptist work existed.

Mary and Davis were appointed with four other missionaries during the first week of May 1951. The 20 who attended were staff and trustees of the Foreign Mission Board. Each new missionary was asked to give a testimony, which really made Mary nervous. She looked around the room and her eyes caught those of a trustee and trusted friend, William Pettigrew. Her heart slowed its pounding. She took a deep breath and began to talk about her call to be a missionary. A dream of many years was finally reality.

For their second day in Richmond, the newly appointed missionaries were given their orientation schedule:

*10:00 A.M.  Everett Dean, treasurer*
*11:00 A.M.  Cotton Wright, business manager*
*12:00 P.M.  Lunch with George Sadler*
*2:00 P.M.   Fon Scofield, communications*

The experience was both relaxing and affirming. The committee looked at their talents and gifts and placed Davis and Mary where they could best serve. Davis's assignment was to be involved in the building and encouraging of local churches. Mary was not given an assignment; her ministry was to be extended only as her home duties permitted. She was encouraged to make the home her priority; and then to reach out to others. Her nursing skills were considered important, but her role of wife and mother was to be her focus.

During this brief time in Richmond, Davis and Mary caught a glimpse of the challenge that lay before them. Their salary, which was called a subsistence allowance, would be sent overseas. Their annual salary of $1,000 would be divided and sent every three months to the Nigerian Baptist mission treasurer in US dollars. He would cash the check and they would receive their money in Nigerian currency.

From the Foreign Mission Board's business manager they learned how to crate and ship household goods overseas. They also learned about their travel arrangements by sea.

Lunch in the hotel with the Sadlers was the highlight of the day. This was when they heard from someone who had actually been to Nigeria. George Sadler freely shared his insights and expectations.

They met with Fon Scofield, who talked to them about taking pictures. He gave them a camera and told them that if they sent back pictures he would send them some new film.

Missionary orientation over, they traveled back to Louisville.

The next day was graduation. The evening after graduation, there was a special dinner for graduates. Davis attended and then earned $5 by washing dishes after the celebration was over.

That week Davis, Mary, and Lee moved back to Charleston to prepare to go to Nigeria. For three months Davis was the interim pastor at Remount Baptist Church. This congregation of 100 had recently purchased a military chapel and was searching for a pastor; but in the meantime, they wanted Davis to lead them. This group of fellow believers affirmed and encouraged Davis and Mary in a time when confidence and support were desperately needed.

Both Davis and Mary's parents were having a difficult time accepting their children's decision to go overseas. Mary's mother was so unhappy at the thought of her six-month-old grandchild being taken from her; her tears fell easily when Mary came to visit. Mary's father was angry. He neither understood nor accepted that his daughter had to leave her family to follow Christ. His response was to ignore her. It was a painful time for Mary. Deep, numbing pain filled and weighed her heart down.

During this time they packed and prepared for departure. After building a crate, they packed a wood stove, a kerosene refrigerator, a mattress and box springs, a case of toilet paper, a case of green beans, a case of peas, and a case of corn. Their order for a hoe, shovel, and rake had not yet come in from Sears so they wrote asking that their order be sent to New Orleans, their port of exit.

They were ready to go.

# CHAPTER 4

# LAGOS, NIGERIA

*"Trust in the Lord with all your heart,*
*And do not lean on your own understanding.*
*In all your ways acknowledge Him,*
*And He will make your paths straight"*

*(Prov. 3:5-6).*

In September 1951, Davis and Mary had made all the necessary preparations and were ready to begin their lives as foreign missionaries. Citadel Square Baptist Church held a farewell service for them, and many tears were shed. Then their plans changed; the freighter they were to travel on was delayed. Another Sunday passed, and again, with many tearful good-byes.

The next week brought an additional delay. Another Sunday arrived, and everyone experienced yet another emotional parting with hugs, kisses, and words of good-bye.

Again, they received word of another delay. Davis hung up the telephone.

"Mary, the freighter has issued an additional delay of one week," he said.

"Oh no," replied Mary. "I don't think I can say good-bye again. I'm emotionally worn out from so many farewells."

And so the following Sunday, the young, soon-to-be missionaries headed to another church for worship.

Finally the following week, they were told that the freighter was almost ready. Taking the few suitcases they owned, they traveled by train to New Orleans and arrived at the port office of the Delta Freight Lines, where they received word of another change.

"I'm sorry, sir," the clerk said, "but the freighter to West Africa left port yesterday."

"Yesterday?" Davis responded in astonishment.

"Yes sir, that's right," replied the clerk.

"But we were told that it would leave today."

"Yes sir, but they were able to finish loading their freight a day early and so they headed to their next stop."

Undaunted by this new twist in their travel arrangements, Davis asked, "Next stop. Where is that?"

"Just a moment and I'll check."

The helpful clerk left for a few minutes and then returned with the news.

"The freighter is headed to Port Arthur, Texas. You can catch up with her there."

Davis and Mary raced for the Greyhound bus station.

"Three tickets for Port Arthur," Davis said.

After their cross-country trip, Mary and Davis gave a sigh of relief to find the large Delta freighter, *Del Rio*, still in dock. They boarded without further delay.

The trip from the US to Nigeria lasted nearly eight weeks—a long and weary journey for the young couple with their infant daughter. Traveling on the same freighter were missionaries Dr. and Mrs. W. L. Jester and John and Niña Mills, returning from furlough.

During the voyage Mary and Davis received practical orientation to missionary life. This was valuable time with their more seasoned colleagues. Among other things, they learned that the country of

Nigeria held one sixth of the continent's population, making it the most populous country in Africa. They also learned that World War II had impacted Nigerian leaders who began presenting ideas of freedom from British colonial rule.

That very year, a new constitution, five years in the making, was put into place. It allowed for elected representation and gave rise to regional political parties. This effort to integrate a country of many tribes and ethnic groups came from a desire to unify an extremely diverse population. Yet, it was this very diversity that threatened the desired unity.

One afternoon as the passengers sat together on the deck, a radio message came. It was delivered to Niña Mills.

Niña sat quietly as she read the news, then handed the telegram to her husband, John.

"Your father has died," was all the brief message said. There was a time of silence, then the group gathered together in prayer for Niña and her family.

Mary sat stunned. Niña's parents had been at the dock in Port Arthur, Texas, to say good-bye to their daughter embarking on a second tour of work in Nigeria.

Deeply saddened by the news, Niña was still able to continue on the journey to Africa. Her serenity and confidence in the face of the dreadful loss, in spite of her inability to be with her family during this time, made a deep impression upon Mary and Davis.

Davis and Mary's exposure to a new and different world was full of strange and wonderful sights and sounds. Being on a freighter meant traveling with many intermediate stops to load or unload the ship's cargo. Their first stop was a port in the Cape Verde Islands.

As they left the ship, Mary commented, "Look at those heavy bags, Davis. What do you think they are?"

"I think they are filled with salt," Davis replied.

"Some of the men look so weak; I don't see how they can carry them," Mary said with sadness.

Just then the foreman callously pushed one of the men off the ramp where he was trampled by his fellow workers.

"Davis, can't you do something?" Mary asked in distress as she saw the man being trampled.

"I think it will just cause even more problems if I try to interfere. We're just visitors here."

Dock after dock, Mary witnessed man's inhumanity to man. In reality she was being exposed to the nature of man around the globe. The voyage seemed endless.

"I think we've only lost two," Mary said.

"Two what?" Davis asked as he watched Mary leaning over the little tub in their cabin to wash diapers.

"Two diapers. I think we've only lost two diapers over the railings when I've hung them out to dry," she replied.

"Is that bad?"

"At this rate, it *will* be a problem before we get to Nigeria. But right now I'm more worried about Lee's health. I think she has pneumonia. Her cough has been getting worse and her fever is going higher."

"What should we do?" asked Davis. He was so glad Mary was a nurse and could handle these kinds of situations.

"Once we get into port tomorrow we need to find some penicillin," Mary answered.

The next day Davis was able to obtain some penicillin and syringes for their young baby. Knowing that now she would often be the only medical person to care for her family, Mary steeled herself and gave her baby daughter the painful injections of penicillin mixed with oil.

For Mary the voyage was especially difficult. As an ex-marine, Davis quickly adjusted to the roll of the sea; but Mary suffered from sea sickness much of the time and had to be confined to their small cabin. The meals on the freighter were another challenge the missionaries faced. To be sure, the garlic meals did not help in her weakness.

"Garlic, garlic, and more garlic. That's all I can taste."

Mary got up to leave the table. She had no appetite and everything was beginning to taste the same—like garlic.

Davis reached over and picked up a toothpick. He began to pick out the large chunks of garlic from his food. The toothpick quickly filled up and there was still more on the plate.

As he showed it to the other passengers he asked, "Do you think it would help Mary if I showed her just why everything tastes like garlic?"

The general consensus was no!

Finally they reached Lagos, Nigeria, the country that was to be their new home. Mary's first impressions were of the masses—people everywhere. She saw that there would be many adjustments to make in the months to come. She felt overwhelmed by this culture, so very different from her own.

The freighter could not dock in Lagos, so a ladder was put over the side of the deck. Mary held her breath as she watched Davis carry Lee in his arms while climbing down into the small launch awaiting them. She followed with her knees shaking and her heart in her throat.

*So different, so different* . . . kept running through her mind.

Cranes were being used to unload their crates. Voices shouted directions in a language she could not understand. Confusion. Chaos.

*So different, so different* . . .

Lavelle Seats met Davis and Mary in Lagos and drove them inland to Ogbomosho, where they would stay with him and his wife, Betty.

Betty waited on the front porch; but as she saw the car coming into the driveway, she ran back in the house and cranked up her old gramophone. The music pealed through the windows as Davis and Mary walked up.

"Carolina Moon keep shining . . . shining on the one who waits for me . . ."

Mary paused as Betty came through the front door.

"I've been saving that record to play for your arrival," Betty announced.

The tears streamed down Mary's cheeks. With the dry dust of travel on her face, the tears made streaks of mud that pooled around her quivering chin. The first touch of the familiar broke down the reserves Mary had built up to deal with all the new and different situations that she had faced over the past few weeks.

Mary sat down on the steps to collect herself as the others went inside. Betty sat down beside her.

"I've been saving something else for you," Betty said.

Mary felt a wet nose against her arm. She looked up to find a young dog, a pointer, nuzzling her.

"It's a gift for you to take to your new home."

Mary found comfort among these new, caring friends, still . . . things were *so different*.

1951: On the way to language school with Lee.

Home at first was Iwo, Nigeria, where they began learning the Yoruba language. Davis and Mary started their language study course three times, for as new students enrolled, their teacher began again from the beginning. After three months of study, they were given their first assignment in Igede. They had only a beginning understanding of Yoruba; the rest they learned as they worked.

Davis was assigned as an area missionary. This meant

extensive travel to the outlying churches for two or three weeks at a time. Initially his trips were even longer because he had so much to learn.

Mary also had an assignment. The Mission had been requesting a nurse for that area for 13 years. So when Mary arrived in Igede, the Nigerians celebrated and many brought gifts. A clinic had been built. It was a mud-walled room with a tin roof, and a large open porch that served as a waiting room. Benches were placed along the walls for seating.

During the first two days that Mary held a clinic she saw 304 patients. As a young nurse she was overwhelmed. Eva Sanders, a missionary nurse in Ire, made the 75-mile trip for the first few days. With her she brought the encouragement of her long experience and lots of written instructions. Mary was thankful for Eva's assistance, knowing that she would not have made it through that first week without the loving support that Eva provided.

In the year that followed, Mary held clinic each morning. She had a helper each day and a midwife, named Banji Adelowa, as part of her team. Banji was a Yoruba woman with traditional markings on her face.

Mary learned that each of the Nigerian tribes had its own tribal markings. The Yoruba markings were three slashes across each cheek. The cuts were made in infancy, with ashes rubbed into the wound to assure a remarkable scarring. Banji, at the age of 30, wore her deep black markings proudly as a reminder of her heritage.

The clinic began each morning with a devotional. Mary always shared openly with the patients that the reason for her being there was her love for Jesus Christ. Banji, also a Christian, served both as interpreter and language teacher for Mary during these sessions.

In 1952, Mary became pregnant with her second child, but she continued the clinic. Mary considered herself fortunate to be able to have her monthly checkups during pregnancy. Fellow missionary, Dr. Edwin Low, visited her clinic once a month to see her most critical patients. After they cared for these patients, Mary would get up on the exam table herself; it was her turn.

During this pregnancy Proverbs 3:5-6 came to mean even more to Mary. With Davis traveling so much, she spent a lot of time alone and for the first time became lonely and homesick. Often during those difficult days of loneliness, she found herself saying over and over again: *"Trust in the Lord with all your heart, And do not lean on your own understanding. In all your ways acknowledge Him, And He will make your paths straight."*

This time, Davis had been gone for two weeks when Mary heard the car pull up to the house. She didn't hear the car door open or shut, so she went out to meet her husband.

*He must be exhausted,* she thought, *He's slumped over the wheel.*

She opened the door to wake him, and he rolled out of the car and fell to the ground. She quickly felt for a pulse. It was weak, but he was still alive. Partly carrying, but mostly dragging him, she pulled Davis into their house and onto the bed. She sent for the pastor and church leaders.

Davis groaned, "Mary, I hurt so bad."

*What to do? What to do!* Mary nervously thought.

She knew that he was seriously ill, but she didn't know what the problem was. He ached all over. Even the light hurt his eyes.

*Morphine.* She had some and maybe that would help him. Her hands were shaking as she went for the medicine.

She gave him a shot, but he continued moaning and crying out, "Mary, I hurt so much."

His pain was more than he could bear—more than even she could bear.

*Maybe I haven't given him enough morphine,* Mary thought. *He is a large man.* So she prepared another shot.

Davis's breathing slowed down . . . and then it slowed down even more. Davis started to turn blue.

"Oh no," she cried out, "I've killed him!"

Mary shook him and his breathing increased. Then, there was a knock on the front door. Several men of the church had come with the pastor.

"Come, pray," cried out Mary, "My husband is dying."

They gathered around him and began to pray.

As they prayed, Mary gathered supplies for the 100-mile trip to the nearest hospital. The men carried Davis to the backseat of the vehicle.

"We will continue to pray," they committed as Mary jumped into the front seat.

Off she went with Davis crying out in pain with each jostle and bump.

*No more morphine for you!* she told herself.

Her hands still shook as she barreled down the road. Turning a corner, she saw that cattle blocked the way. To avoid an accident she swerved to the left, bounced off the road and drove through a field. She was finally forced to stop as the cattle and oxen surrounded her and created an impasse.

"Mary!" Davis cried out.

She turned around to see her husband trying to speak.

"Where are we? Why are you back here?" he said.

With the window down, a cow had stuck its head inside the back and was peering down at Davis with a great deal of curiosity. He squinted because the light caused him such severe pain, and in the haze of his illness he thought it was Mary leaning over him.

"It's all right, Davis," she tried to reassure him while giving the curious cow a shove out of the window, "We're going to be at the hospital soon."

"Dengue fever," diagnosed the physician when they arrived.

"What can we do to treat it?" asked Mary.

"Pain relief and rest is all that we know to do; just . . ."

"I know," stated Mary, "be careful with the pain relief!"

It was many weeks before Davis was able to move around and begin to work again. The fear that had clutched at Mary's heart passed, and she was even able to kid him.

"Davis, do you know how I knew you were *really* sick?"

She paused for effect.

"You let me drive the car, and didn't say one thing about my driving all the way to Ogbomosho," she joked.

It was no secret that Mary had a penchant for getting lost, and for knowing little about operating cars. Their car was an older British model called an Anglia. The gears were worn and had a tendency to slip. Davis spent a good deal of time teaching Mary what to do when the gears slipped out of place and the car was rendered useless.

Although Davis knew his wife's mechanical knowledge was limited, she had fooled the rest of the village. How impressed they were that first day the car had stalled while she was driving!

*Stay calm,* she told herself, *You know what to do.*

She hopped out of the driver's seat and moved to the back of the car. Opening up the "boot" she hauled out a toolbox and brought it around to the front of the car. A crowd was gathering, obviously impressed, as intended, with her mechanical know-how.

She carefully selected a wrench and tucked her head under the hood of the car.

*Let's see, where did he tell me to hit so that I would knock the gears back into place?* Mary thought, concentrating on her task.

"There, that ought to do it," she said with a confident voice, as she whacked at a gear and saw it slip back into line.

Putting her "tools" away, she jumped back in the car and prepared to continue. The crowd around her clapped. They were obviously impressed.

"That woman, did you see her?" asked one man, in wonder.

"Yes, she knows much about cars," responded his friend.

"I have never seen a woman fix cars!" remarked a third.

"So good, so good," remarked another, knowingly.

With Davis recuperating from dengue fever, Mary resumed her daily clinic hours, even though she was now becoming heavy with her unborn child. Each morning she had a steep hill to walk down in order to get to the clinic. One morning, however, during the rainy season, she slipped and fell. Dr. Low recommended that she not travel the hill to the clinic until after the baby was born. She didn't, but that didn't close the clinic. It was just moved up to her front porch until the beginning of her ninth month.

When it was time for the arrival of her second child, she and Davis went to stay in Ogbomosho until she delivered a daughter, Susan Danner, in the hospital on October 31, 1952.

After Danner's birth the women in Igede were very excited about Mary's new baby coming home. And so, one morning Mary laid Danner in the center of the room on a blanket and hundreds of women came by to meet her. Each of them brought a fresh egg for they all knew how much Mary loved eggs. Fresh eggs were not easy to get. They had all seen her at the market using her flashlight to look at the eggs trying to get those that were not so close to becoming little chicks.

As the line of women was coming to an end, Mary saw one of her friends. "Thank you for coming," she said.

"I have brought a pencil and paper," said her friend. "But it is a gift for me and not for you. Please write down everything you do for I want my baby to be just like that one!"

Mary smiled.

One day Mrs. Fatunla came to visit Mary. This short, wiry, dynamic leader was the pastor's wife of the Baptist church in Igede. She was also the regional leader for women's work. Her theme was "Each one, teach one."

If she found someone who could read and write, she immediately made plans for that person to teach another who could not.

"Come walk with me," she said to Mary.

They went on a walk toward the marketplace. As they walked Mrs. Fatunla began gathering people together to meet her new friend. Many people came together quickly and when there was a big enough crowd, Mrs. Fatunla turned to Mary and said, "You may speak now."

Taking a deep breath Mary began quoting from John 8:32, "You shall know the truth, and the truth shall make you free." Standing in the open-air market center, Mary felt the wind as it blew her hair gently across her face. She felt the sunshine beaming down. But greater still, she felt that sense of belonging, of being where she should be. She knew without a doubt that she spoke the truth and in that truth she felt the freedom to share the things of her heart.

At the end of each month Davis held a pastor's school on their front porch. There were seven students. One of these students was named Ogundano. He was a young man, still single, but known for his sweet spirit and gentle ways. After class one day he asked to speak to Mary.

"I would like for you to look at my foot," asked Ogundano. "I have had a sore on it that will not heal."

As Mary looked at his foot she felt sure she knew what the problem was.

"Ogundano," she said, "I would like for you to come next week when Dr. Low comes. I think he should look at this before we decide what to do."

When Dr. Low came he sadly confirmed Mary's diagnosis. It was difficult news for a young missionary nurse to give to a young and eager pastor.

"Ogundano, your foot shows that you have leprosy," Mary told the young Nigerian as tears welled up in her eyes.

"This means that I will have to go to the leper colony to live, doesn't it?"

"Yes, I'm afraid it does," Mary responded sadly.

Several months later Mary received a letter from him.

He wrote, "I would rather be a leper and know Christ than be a whole person and not know my Lord and Savior."

Ogundano took his faith to the leper colony. Trained as a pastor, it was there he preached and told of the hope to be found in Christ. It was there he planted Christ's church.

After their first year in Igede, Mary and Davis were asked by the mission board to move to Iwo. They lived there for two years and taught students. Mary and Davis rode bicycles as their means of transportation—she rode hers to the clinic and he rode his to the school. At the end of the day they would meet and pedal home together.

In Igede, Mary held clinic, this time with missionary nurse Hazel Moon. Davis was the one who took the critical patients to the hospital in Ogbomosho: morning, noon, or night.

After seeing a sick patient early one morning, Mary woke Davis up and asked, "Davis, would you like to go to the hospital in Ogbomosho?"

Davis sat up straight in the bed and responded, "Mary, don't wake me up at 3:00 A.M. to ask me if I want to go to Ogbomosho. No, I don't want to go; but if you need me to, I will. Just don't offer me a choice."

Davis and Mary helped each other whenever they could. They were a team. One night when a man's leg was badly cut, Davis held the lantern so Mary could have enough light to work by. Her slightly shaking hands were the only indication that these were the first sutures she had ever put in. Nursing in Nigeria was a far cry from the training she had received at Roper Hospital. Often Mary would call upon the Great Physician to give her peace and calmness as she faced new medical crises for which she was not prepared.

"If I can learn how to sew a man's leg, I can learn how to sew clothes," declared Mary. "How hard can it be?"

Inspired to learn a new craft, Mary borrowed a treadle sewing machine and a pattern for men's pajamas. Soon she was busy at work, cutting and sewing the new blue cotton material she had purchased at the market.

"No, that doesn't look right," she admitted as she held up the pants. "I'll have to rip the seam out and try again."

As Mary picked out the newly sewn seam, for the fifth or sixth time, she acknowledged that sewing was a little harder than she had anticipated. Davis's new pajamas looked like an unusual long skirt; somehow there was no crotch.

Finally in frustration she asked for help.

"Davis, I am not doing very well. Do you think you could help me?"

With his civil engineering background, Davis began, "OK, Mary, let's look at the blueprints."

"Do you mean the pattern instructions?" Mary asked.

"That's it."

Working together, the pajamas were finally finished. There was only one flaw. The front seam of the pants had been stitched and ripped so many times that the material finally gave way. There was a hole where the fly should have been.

"Don't worry, Mary," comforted her husband, "I'll only wear these when we're at home. No one else will see them. And plus, I won't have to pull down my pants when I want to go to the bathroom."

Together they laughed long and loud.

"You'll get better with time," Davis assured her.

And she did!

In Iwo Mary and Davis became expectant parents for the third time. Davis traveled a lot during this time and he cautioned Mary to always lock up the house at night. He knew that she had a bad habit of forgetting. One morning she awoke with a start in the early hours of the morning just before dawn. Someone was in the kitchen and it was obvious from the noise that the person was in the process of removing all of her dishes.

*What should I do?* she wondered. She feared for the safety of her unborn child and her two little daughters asleep in the next room.

Several minutes passed, but the banging and removal of pots

and pans did not cease. Finally she undid the mosquito netting that covered her bed and weakly called out, "Davis?" She hoped that in calling her husband's name she would scare the thief away. She repeated herself a little louder, "Davis?"

From the kitchen came a voice, "Yes, Mary?" Arriving home at 4:00 A.M. Davis discovered that millions of deadly army ants had invaded the kitchen in search of food. He was trying to divert their trail out of the house. He had recently seen these ants kill a 400-pound hog by covering it and eating it alive!

In April 1954, as the time for Mary's third delivery drew near, she kept a bag, full of everything she might need when the time came, ready. The hospital was 57 miles away over a deeply-rutted, dirt-packed road. The day her labor began, she, Davis, and Hazel Moon began the trip. Each bump and rut only served to increase her labor pains, and Davis was torn between trying to go faster in order to arrive sooner or trying to go slower to avoid triggering more contractions. All three of them were relieved to reach the hospital in Ogbomosho.

In the delivery room, Dr. Ed Low prepared the anesthesia to

1954: Mary with Nigerian pastors in Oshogbo.

help her with her pain; but after a few minutes she cried out, "Ed, the anesthesia is not helping."

Calmly he replied, "Breathe it in, Mary, you're just not getting enough . . ."

She responded, "But it's not helping."

"Just breathe in."

And so she did—great big gulps of air. The pain remained.

Finally John Alva Lee Saunders II was born, proudly named after Davis's father.

Several minutes later Dr. Low came sheepishly to Mary's side. "Mary, I need to apologize," he said. "I'm sorry. I just discovered that I forgot to turn on the anesthesia gas. All I was giving you was oxygen! You were right, it probably wasn't helping your pain a whole lot. But with all that oxygen, John's coloring looks great!"

As an infant, John developed large sores. Mary treated him for impetigo, but the sores kept getting worse and worse. Finally, she took a needle and popped one area, and a black-headed worm wiggled out. Soon she had 17 such worms in a matchbox.

"I don't know what this is, but I'm going to find out," Mary said aloud.

With that declaration, Mary drove 50 miles to the leper colony to talk with a doctor there.

"Tumbu fly," was the doctor's response. "The flies come from the mango trees and they plant their eggs under the skin. Some call them mango flies. The eggs eat at body tissue to grow and survive."

"But how can I prevent them?"

"The flies often place their eggs in damp clothing; and then when they are next to the skin, the eggs implant themselves under the skin. Heat will kill them."

"You mean if I iron everything thoroughly . . ."

"Yes, that will help."

And so, from 7:00 P.M. to 9:00 P.M. when there was electricity, Mary ironed all of John's clothes, particularly his diapers. And, on the days when no electricity came, she placed a solid, nonelectric iron in her out-side fire and killed any mango flies that might dare come her way.

While the sores from the mango flies were still healing, John became critically ill. His temperature soared and then dropped, soared and dropped. In between the fevers, his little body shook with chills. Mary knew this was malaria. She prepared an injection of penicillin and quinoquin. She was careful about the dose, fearful of giving him too much of the potent antimalarial.

Still his condition worsened. So once again, they drove to the hospital in Ogbomosho.

"Mary, John has cerebral malaria. We don't know if he will make it. He's pretty critical," shared one of the doctors.

Throughout the night two doctors stayed awake while guarding this little boy's life. In the morning his fever began to recede. The worst was over.

Not long after this, the five Saunderses left Iwo for their sched-uled furlough in the US.

In 1955, after a year of furlough, Davis and Mary returned once again to Nigeria. This time the Nigerian Mission asked them to live in Oshogbo in order for Davis to be mission builder for a year. Their home in Oshogbo had few amenities: mud walls with a tin roof, no electricity, no screens or glass in the windows, and no running water. The water was hauled from nine miles away.

To carry the water Davis built a large tank that fit onto a trailer. Each week he hooked the trailer up to the car and collected their water supply. Returning home from filling the tank he backed the trailer up in a narrow space between the side of the house and a large tree. On the large tree he built a second tank. Fastened to the side of the tree was a hand pump which was used to bring the water from the trailer to the tree. A hose was connected from the tank into the bathroom window.

"Davis," Mary called, when tanks and pump were complete and installed.

She filled up a bucket from the hose coming in the bathroom window, and began to jog across the courtyard to the kitchen area. Water sloshed on her legs as she ran.

Davis reached the doorway. She met him with a grin.

"We have running water!"

Davis encouraged Mary as she tried to learn how to back up the trailer, "You see, it's not that difficult!"

"It's no use. I just can't remember which way to turn the thing. I jackknife the trailer every time."

Secretly Davis thought she had a good point. He just didn't want to admit it aloud.

"I hate to leave you for this trip. I know you'll need more water before I get back," he said.

"Don't worry. I'll figure out a way," Mary replied.

It certainly wasn't from a lack of trying on Mary's part, but when Davis returned from that trip, and many others, he always found the water trailer in the front of the house, and the tank in the tree dry.

"How did you do with getting water?" he asked.

"Well, I couldn't go backward so I made sure I could always go forward!"

Mary kept the trailer tank filled as needed, but only had "running" water when Davis was around. She never accomplished the art of backing up a trailer.

During this time Davis was building their own mission home. Eagerly Mary watched the bricks being made and dried in the sun. It was a beautiful place of which they were extremely proud. Finally they were able to move into their new home.

One day, sitting on the front porch, Mary prayed. "Lord, I feel as though I have arrived. I love living here. You're going to have to call long and hard to move me from Oshogbo." Everything seemed tailor-made to her gifts and talents. She was working in a clinic with Eva Sanders, who she loved dearly. A local Muslim school allowed her to teach there and she started a Christian Student Union among these young men.

Davis, in addition to his responsibilities as mission builder, was the associational mission advisor. Once a month he invited all of the pastors from the association to their home for a meal and a meeting. For the first meeting in their new home, Mary was excited. The house was finally ready to receive guests. Before leaving the US, she and Davis had even been given two beautiful carpets which were now in the living room and dining room.

As the pastors arrived both Mary and Davis noted to their dismay that each man carefully removed his shoes as he entered their beautiful rooms. It was clear that these men were uncomfortable walking on the carpets. The second month's meeting came and as the pastors arrived they saw there was no need to remove their shoes. The carpets had long since been rolled up and given away. Although Davis and Mary loved beautiful things, they had no desire to allow possessions to interfere with their ministry.

That same year George Sadler, area director for the Foreign Mission Board, came for a visit. He had one surprise key question for them. "What would you think of going to Tanganyika[1] to begin a new work?"

"If I knew where it was and how to spell it I might consider it," was Davis's lighthearted response.

George Sadler was in earnest though, and several weeks after his visit a letter arrived. There was a request for Davis, Wimpy Harper, and Jack Walker to take a trip to East Africa and survey the land. They planned a six-week trip across continent to the eastern part of Africa.

While Davis was gone, Mary spent much time in prayer. She was so happy in Oshogbo. She loved the people, the culture, and the way of life. Was she ready to go if God were to lead them to East Africa? She wasn't sure.

During this time the first organizational meeting was held for the All Africa Baptist Women. Knowing of Mary's beautiful soprano voice they asked her to sing one evening for the worship service. The song they chose for her was "Wherever He Leads I'll Go."

Standing before all those women, she began to sing,

"Wherever he leads I'll go.

Wherever he leads I'll go . . ."

Her voice began to waver as she sensed the impact of the words on her own life.

"I'll follow my Christ who loves me so."

The lump in her throat was too big; she couldn't finish the song. Finally she sat down with tears pouring down her cheeks. Mrs. Edgar Bates, president of the Baptist Women came to her, put her arms around her, and asked, "Just where is it that you are going, my dear?"

Through her tears Mary replied, "I'm going to East Africa."

Quietly that woman of God laid her hands on Mary and prayed, "The Lord bless you and keep you. The Lord make His face to shine upon you and give you peace."

After that night, peace is what Mary felt as she made her plans to move to East Africa. When Davis returned, she knew already and was prepared for the fact that it was time for a move. She had lived in the house that Davis built them[2] for three months.

---

[1]Tanganyika became the modern African country of Tanzania in 1964.

[2] Today the house still stands. It belongs to the Nigerian Baptist Convention. Even after many years it is called the *Saunders'* house.

# CHAPTER 5

# NAIROBI, KENYA

*"That He would grant you, according to the riches of
His glory, to be strengthened with power through
His Spirit in the inner man"*

*(Eph. 3:16).*

On the porch of their home in Oshogbo, Nigeria, Mary and Davis prayed and planned with four others: Jack and Sally Walker, and Wimpy and Juanita Harper. These three couples were to be the beginning of the Baptist Mission of East Africa. They elected a chairman, secretary, and treasurer. They then developed 12 committees! Everyone had plenty of jobs to do.

As they met, it was apparent that one couple needed to go to the United States and share in detail their plans with those at the Foreign Mission Board. Davis and Mary were asked to go first to Virginia and then fly to Dar es Salaam. The other two couples would proceed on to Tanganyika immediately. After the East African survey trip, it was clear that Tanganyika was the country in which to start work. In Uganda the men had received opposition from the Anglican Church of Uganda. In Kenya, the leaders of the Christian Council of Kenya had said that they were not interested. And so, plans were made for the work to begin first in Tanganyika.

In the original plans, Davis and Mary were to move to the town of Mbeya to work with Jack and Sally Walker. However, shortly after their arrival in Dar es Salaam, their plans were revised—once again. Other missionaries were coming. The Christian Council of Kenya now offered an invitation for Baptists to enter Kenya, and Davis and Mary were the ones chosen to answer that invitation.

On December 12, 1956, Davis drove to Nairobi in a newly purchased Land Rover with one-and-a-half-year-old John. Later that week, Mary, pregnant with their fourth child, flew with the two girls, now ages five and three. They all arrived in Nairobi on December 17. No one knew them or knew of their arrival in Kenya.

For the first several weeks, "home" was the Norfolk Hotel in downtown Nairobi. One of the first of many dilemmas was money.

1956: The first missionaries of the East African Mission. Top row, l to r: Wimpy Harper, Davis Saunders, and Jack Walker. Bottom row, l to r: Juanita Harper, Mary Saunders, and Sally Walker. This picture was taken in Nigeria just before they left for East Africa.

It would take several days before the local bank could verify their records and cash a check. As Christmas drew closer they feared that they would run out of money. However, the day before Christmas, the authorization came and they were able to get some cash. With some of this money Davis and Mary bought each of the children a gift. They did not have the time or money for a Christmas tree, so the gifts were hidden in the Land Rover until the next morning. Still, Christmas came to the Norfolk Hotel that year.

On New Year's Eve, however, the manager of the Norfolk informed them that they had stayed at the hotel beyond the limit for patrons. Thus, after securing two rooms at the Fairview Hotel, they moved again.

During this time, Davis searched for housing. At the end of January they were able to purchase a house on the edge of the Ngong Hills forest. The owner and builder, Mr. Moore, was an Englishman. He had come to East Africa to retire. The desire of his later life was to have peace and quiet and to spend time leisurely reading the daily paper. Much to his chagrin he realized that the local paper, *The East African Standard*, took, at most, 15 minutes to read. As for peace and quiet, there had been political turmoil since he had arrived in this country. After selling his house, he returned to England, wishing this young couple well.

The house was not quite finished, but the Saunders family moved in regardless. It was built on an empty lot with no grass. The red clay dirt covered everything, both inside and out. Soon after moving in Mary purchased some grass seeds and started planting, trying to bend down over her ever-growing abdomen. As always, she was determined to make her home as pleasant as possible.

Once they were settled, Davis began to travel a great deal, trying to learn about this beautiful country, trying to understand the people and their needs. He knew that other Baptist missionaries would come soon and he wanted to understand where the greatest needs were.

This was not a stable time for the country of Kenya, which had been a British colony since 1895. The winds of change were blowing across this fertile land. Since 1928, Jomo Kenyatta had been a full-time official representing Kenyans in protesting against the "white settlers." Historically the British government had been more concerned with their own gains rather than the gains and rights of the African people.

In the early 1950s, the Kikuyu led a revolt which culminated in the Mau Mau rebellion. The Kikuyu refused to acknowledge any loss of their original lands to Europeans. The rebellion did not spread among other Kenyan peoples, but many Kikuyu lives were lost. Few white settlers lost their lives in this rebellion. Many of the rebels were placed in detention camps near Nairobi in 1954. Jomo Kenyatta was captured and imprisoned because of his part in the rebellion. In 1956 policies were put in place which favored majority rule of Kenya and independence.

However, as Davis and Mary moved into their new home, Kenyatta remained in detention. Plans for Kenyan independence were hampered by the Kenya African National Union, the major political party in Kenya which refused to cooperate completely until Kenyatta was released. Tensions and unrest continued.

Mary sat in the living room and turned on the "wireless." Davis was traveling again and she wanted to hear the latest news.

"And now the latest in Kenya," said the announcer.

Mary listened carefully.

"There is a warning in effect for those living in the Ngong Hills district. It is recommended that they use extreme caution and lock their homes securely. Ten prisoners have escaped from the government detention camps in that area and are still said to be nearby.

An English woman who lived in this area was found murdered this morning. Her body had multiple knife wounds. Officials are stating that the death was clearly done by the escaped prisoners."

As she turned the wireless off, Mary was reminded again that it was not a good time to be one with white skin in this fledgling nation.

She remembered this past week when she had gone on a walk around her neighborhood.

"*Jambo,*" she greeted those she passed by, hoping to start a conversation.

The women looked away.

A little farther on she tried again.

"*Jambo.*"

The response came, "*Jambo,*" but the tone of voice showed anger and contempt.

After a few minutes of walking she tried again.

"*Jambo, habari yako?*" (Hello, how are you?)

The woman who she smiled at looked at her and then slowly turned and spit on the ground at Mary's feet.

When Mary returned to the house Davis saw tears in her eyes.

"Oh, Davis, they hate us here. They make it so clear that they don't want us here. Why did we leave Nigeria to come to this? In Oshogbo the people loved us. I was needed in the clinic, you were needed in the church work. Why has God brought us to this land?"

As the words tumbled out, Davis listened and said nothing. He knew her frustration; he had no simple answers.

Davis was becoming acquainted with many of the government officials as he met with them to apply for registration of the Baptist Mission and also to receive permission to own property.

One evening, Mr. Purvis, secretary of the legislative council in Nairobi, invited the Saunderses to dinner at the "Chambers." Davis and Mary were delighted, although Mary was a little anxious because she was very nauseated a good deal of the time with this pregnancy. In fact, she carried a brown bag with her everywhere.

That evening the four-course meal began with kidney consommé. Mary looked down at the little pieces of kidney floating in the pale yellow liquid and knew she was in trouble. As graciously as she could she asked her oh-so-proper British hostess if there was a "powder room." There was, right next to the dining room.

As she vomited again and again she wondered if she could be heard in the adjoining room.

Her worst fears were confirmed when she returned to the table.

Davis's face was beet red and he whispered, "Isn't there any way you could have been quieter?"

In spite of her dignified surroundings, Mary responded, "Davis, just how do you puke quietly?"

After all the proper forms were completed, permission was granted for the Saunderses to begin work. First they went to the office of Mayor I. Soman.

"Yes," said the mayor, "I heard that you Baptists were beginning to work here. How can I help you?"

"We are hoping to find some land to start a church."

"I am afraid I don't have good news. All of the plots designated by the city planners for churches have already been given out."

"Do you have any suggestions about what we can do?"

"We do have one rather large plot that has not yet been claimed," began Soman, "But it is not for a church. It is for a community center."

Davis thought for a few minutes. "We might be interested in beginning there," he said.

"In fairness I must first of all tell you about the location of the land. It is in the district of Shauri Moya. Are you familiar with that area?"

Davis was.

Shauri Moya was one of two areas in the city where the blacks had to live. It was surrounded by a double row of 12-foot barbed wire. There was only one gate to enter the area and it was heavily guarded. One needed a special permit to enter. During these times of political tension all Africans, no matter what tribe, had to live behind the barbed wire. It was to this area that Davis and Mary went.

While work began at Shauri Moya, Davis and Mary also started ministries in other areas outside the city limits. Other missionaries came to Kenya at this time: Sammy and Teeny Debord, Earl and Jane

Martin, James and Gena Hampton. Plus, three more couples were preparing to come.

As new missionaries continued to come, Mary and Davis enjoyed building new friendships. Many stayed with them as they got settled. At one time there were two families staying with them at the same time. That night Mary put all of the children in the first bedroom and one couple in the second bedroom. The second couple slept on the sleeper sofa in the living room.

During the dark, moonless night one of the visiting children couldn't sleep. Going into the bedroom where her parents were, she woke up her mom.

"I'm scared," she cried. "It's too dark here."

"It's OK," said her mom. "You sleep with Dad while I go sleep in your bed with one of the kids."

The house became quiet again.

Later that same night another restless child awoke and went to where her parents were sleeping on the sofa in the living room.

"Dad, I can't sleep."

"You sleep with Mom," was her dad's drowsy reply, "I'll go sleep in your bed with one of the kids."

Early the next morning, screams from the kids' room woke everyone in the house. What could it be? Davis and Mary went running. There they saw the two parents who had moved during the night. They awoke, horrified to find themselves in bed face to face, but not spouse to spouse!

Construction began at Shauri Moya, and Davis and Mary announced that they would begin to hold Sunday services in a nearby nursery school. They also said that there would be Sunday School. They bought a mimeograph machine and the Martins and the Saunderses wrote a Sunday School lesson.

It was hard work, and took hours to do initially. The lesson was written in English first, and then translated into Swahili. Then Mary Smythe, one of their language teachers, corrected it. Finally, it was typed and copies were made.

They knew that all of their efforts were worthwhile as they watched eight children arrive on Sunday morning. Three adults joined them. David Kimilo, Davis's language teacher, would not agree to translate a sermon. He told Davis if he was going to begin preaching he should begin in Swahili. And so Davis preached in Swahili—for three minutes. Then he was finished. He couldn't give an invitation because he hadn't learned those words yet. They sang only a few choruses because there were no hymn books. In all, Sunday School and worship lasted for 15 minutes. Baptist ministry in Nairobi had begun.

With the beginning of new work, Sundays were a busy day. Often co-workers such as Bwana[1] Daniel Mathuku or Elizabeth Wanjiru would go with the Saunders family to the various worship services and Sunday School classes.

When asked where she went on Sundays, Elizabeth answered, "I go to church. We leave Shauri Moya at 8:00 to go to Ngong Hills for a worship service, then on to Athi River at 9:30, then a service at Riruta at 10:30, then back to Shauri Moya by 11:30."

"I've never seen churches in those places," said her friend.

"Well, there aren't buildings yet. We have rented some rooms. Or, like in Ngong Hills, we have permission to meet in a social center. In Riruta we meet in a nursery school."

"You said a social center in Ngong. What is a social center?"

"The Saunderses call it that so they don't have to tell everyone that they are meeting in a bar."

"I can see why."

Another Sunday ritual came in the evenings.

"You're the best chigger-digger in the world, Dad," said Lee.

"Chigger-digger, huh? I don't know if that is in my job description."

After busy Sundays, Mary and the children returned home and searched for little worms called chiggers that buried themselves under the skin to lay their eggs. Sunday evening was the time to dig them out!

In July of that first year, the time came for the arrival of their new baby. Mary had a rough delivery and was quite ill in the Princess Elizabeth Hospital, a two-story nursing home. She never had easy deliveries, but this one was especially difficult.

One of her concerns with this fourth child was that it appeared that Davis had lost interest in her. He rarely came to see her in the hospital and seemed tired and distracted while he was there.

Finally she confronted him.

"Davis, what's wrong? You don't seem interested in me anymore," she said, and the tears began to fall.

Davis looked as though he was trying hard to carefully pick his words.

*What could he be trying to tell me?* Mary wondered.

"Mary, something else happened the night that Niña was born. The doctor has told me that I should not tell you because you have been so sick yourself. Now I see that I must tell you."

"What is it? Please tell me."

"The night Niña was born, Danner was rushed to the hospital for an emergency appendectomy. She was very sick."

"How is she now?"

"She is doing much better. She is in Gertrude Gardens Hospital, 15 miles away. Her visiting hours are the same as yours so I have been running between two hospitals, plus trying to take care of Lee and John at home. Mary, it's not that I'm not interested in you, it's just that there is not enough of me to go around."

As Davis had predicted, Mary got out of the bed.

"Take me to Gertrude Gardens Children's Hospital."

After spending visiting hours with Danner, Mary returned to her own hospital bed to rest and nurse Niña. She continued this until she, Niña, and Danner were all well enough to return home.

British Baptists began to meet for tea one Sunday afternoon each month. On one occasion, Davis and Mary invited their new friends to their home. They didn't own a stove or refrigerator yet, so Mary

1962: Mary vamps for the camera after the wedding of a friend at Riruta Baptist Church in Nairobi, Kenya.

cooked on an electric hot plate for 30 guests. As they visited, Davis challenged these Baptists to begin to worship as well as meet for tea. That Sunday afternoon they committed to begin a Baptist Fellowship. The next month they met for worship and decided to meet weekly in Bible study. As the group grew, they used various buildings in town until at last they were able to purchase a lot and build the Nairobi Baptist Church.

Language study continued for Mary and Davis. Their ministry was so limited without the knowledge of Swahili and they knew they must continue to learn. Toward the end of language school Mary thought she was beginning to do quite well.

One day they were given a test when they arrived. To her dismay the test was to translate portions of the Book of John into English from Swahili. Determined, she began by reading in Swahili.

"Look at the Son of a sheep of God's Who gets the sin of the universe," Mary translated for, "Behold, the Lamb of God who takes away the sin of the world!" (John 1:29*b*).

She knew it didn't sound quite right, but that was the best she could come up with!

As Mary went to each of the new areas where Baptist work was beginning, she looked for one woman in particular who could be her guide and helper as she taught Bible studies, literacy, and sewing. One such woman was Gladys Kimiti. On occasion Davis went with

1963: Mary and the Muslim friend who gave her this "buibui" dress.

Mary to teach the women. On these days, Mary asked the women to invite their husbands. Gladys brought her husband, Peter, and soon they both began to attend the Sunday worship services. As they spent time together a friendship developed.

One day Gladys came for tea. Mary invited her to sit in the living room.

"I'll go fix the tea," Mary said.

As Mary turned and headed toward the kitchen she saw Gladys stand back up.

"Have a seat, Gladys, I'll go fix the tea."

Again Mary started to the kitchen, and again Gladys stood.

"Gladys, I'll be right back. I want to serve you some tea."

"But," Gladys faltered, "I have been watching and those who are your friends sit with you in the kitchen to drink tea. I don't want to be a guest; I want to be a friend."

Arms around each other, the "friends" headed toward the kitchen.

One rainy day Gladys came with tears in her eyes.

"One of my children has just died and I don't even know what was wrong," she wept.

Mary put her arms around her friend and they sat together for some time.

"How can we help?"

"Just sit with me."

After a little while Gladys was ready to return home. Davis and

Mary went with her and met Peter there. He had prepared the body and placed it in a small wooden box.

"Can you help us bury our child?" he asked. "It is a holiday today, so there is no one working that can help us."

Davis carried the small box to the Volkswagen van that they drove, and together they went to the cemetery. The cemetery was empty. No one was there because of the holiday, but several graves had been dug in preparation.

The rain fell and dirt began to cave in on the sides of the graves. Davis, not having a shovel, took the hubcaps off the wheels of his van to dig out the moist soil. Then, together they laid the child in the grave and covered his body with the caked red soil. Davis performed the burial service as the others stood solemnly by. After covering the body, Davis used the hubcaps again to mark the grave and to keep wild dogs from digging up the freshly buried body.

Mary's friendship with Gladys deepened that day. It was just

The Saunders family in 1972. Top row, l to r: Davis, Mary, Lee, bottom row, l to r: Danner, Niña, John.

the beginning. In years to come, Peter became a pastor and was the one to baptize Davis and Mary's youngest daughter, Niña, into new life with Christ.

Shared pain binds people together; shared joy seals those very bonds into true friendship.

Mary's perspective on life was constantly challenged as her new friends shared their lives with her. This was a culture where a man could have more than one wife. In fact, taking a second wife was a declaration of a man's wealth, and an insurance of being cared for in old age.

Gloria was one of Mary's friends. Gloria's burden was that she had remained childless. Her husband, Joshua, was a good man; but as the years went by and Gloria bore him no children, he saw that it was now time to take a second wife.

Gloria and Mary spoke of these things as Gloria shared her husband's plans.

"So, it is planned. His new wife will be much younger than I. I have heard she is a good girl."

"But Gloria," Mary asked in wonder, "what are you going to do when Joshua brings home a new wife?"

"I have prayed about this, and I know what I must do. I must tell this young girl about the Jesus Who has changed my life."

Mary was humbled beyond words.

As Mary spent more time with her Kenyan friends, she began to understand the culture around her. Greetings were so important and could last for several minutes before one could go on with the business at hand. Respect of the elderly and of men was inherent. In general, women gained their role in the community through the birth of their children, especially sons. Because of this, a woman would be renamed after her firstborn son.

In keeping with this tradition, Mary became known as Mama John. Proudly she used her new name for, after all, her only son

John was very special to her. Her new name, Mama John, remained with Mary for the rest of her ministry in Africa.

---

[1]*Bwana* is a Swahili word for *master* or *boss*.

# CHAPTER 6

# ARUSHA, TANZANIA

*"How lovely on the mountains Are the feet of him
who brings good news, Who announces peace And
brings good news of happiness, Who announces
salvation, And says to Zion, 'Your God reigns!'"*

*(Isa. 52:7).*

On the slopes of Mount Meru, in the shadow of Mount
Kilimanjaro, is the Baptist Theological Seminary of East Africa.
Ten miles from the town of Arusha, Tanganyika, the seminary was
founded in 1962 as the need for trained pastors increased. Pastors
and their families came for three years of study.

When Mary and Davis returned to Africa in 1964, Davis became
the principal of this institution. At the time the student body consisted of 30 men, 20 of whom had brought their wives.

In 1964, the country of Tanganyika and the island of Zanzibar
were united, forming what is now known as the country of
Tanzania. The new nation of Tanzania gained independence, led by
Julius Nyerere, president for life, and chairman of the one existing
political party.

Overnight the Baptist Mission ceased to own the 100-acre seminary property; they became tenants, allowed to lease the land. The new government gained ownership. Once again Mama John and her family were living in a country undergoing massive political changes. Their bags packed and ready to go, the family was prepared to leave at a moment's notice should these changes prove threatening.

Under the new principles of African socialism, the government controlled all aspects of economic life. Tanzanians were resettled into "planned villages" and were forced into a collective lifestyle of living and working.

The closest neighbors to the seminary were Americans Bill and Allison Kneib. They owned an extensive coffee plantation that Allison had inherited from her grandfather, who purchased the land while hunting in East Africa with Teddy Roosevelt. This was the only life that Allison knew, and yet she and her husband both saw that they must leave.

Before leaving, Allison gave Mama John a gift—a wrought iron table that had been given to her grandfather by Ernest Hemingway's family. As they said their farewells, Mama John thought back to a tea party Allison once held.

Several women were invited to "tea" because an English visitor, Ann Jakes, had arrived in Tanzania for a visit.

To properly make tea, loose tea leaves are placed in a ceramic teapot with boiling water poured on top. After steeping, the tea is poured into cups through a strainer. Small leaf fragments always pass through the strainer and settle to the bottom of the cup.

"My dears," the guest from England said, "I have learned how to read the tea leaves in the bottom of the teacups."

With this statement, she proceeded to go around the room, giving them bits of humor and pseudo-advice from her tea-reading insights. When she came to Mama John she took her cup and swirled the leaves around and around.

"Such a pure life . . ." Ann sighed, "but so terribly boring!"

As Mama John hugged Allison good-bye she thought, *Boring is the last word I would use to describe this life!*

Quietly the Kneibs packed their car with those things that they held most dear, and drove to the nearest border, never to return. They were good friends to the Saunderses and would be missed.

The political life of Tanzania began to settle, and routines were reestablished. Mama John taught classes at the seminary and often joked about how nice it was to have her husband as her boss. The classes Mama John taught were for the wives of the seminary students. She also held a clinic each morning for those living on the seminary campus. However, as time passed, she saw the need to begin another clinic in a village on the side of Mount Meru. She received governmental permission and permission from the principal of the seminary to have relief from some of her seminary duties for one day a week.

Each Wednesday morning Mama John led a clinic and a Bible study among the Waarusha people, a subtribe of the Maasai. As she drove up the narrow footpath she often passed the young shepherd boys. This particular Wednesday, she took a friend with her.

"What is your name?" she asked a young shepherd one day.

The young boy silently stared at this white woman, his eyes wide with fear and uncertainty.

"You do a good job watching your sheep and goats," Mama John tried again, hoping to begin a conversation.

The young boy remained overwhelmed but his fear was quickly disappearing. He liked the look in this woman's eyes. He saw that she meant him no harm.

Mama John smiled at this raggedly-clothed boy. She knew his responsibility was to tend to the family's herd of sheep and goats. Equipped only with a staff, he guided the flock each day to grass and water.

"I will travel here each week in my vehicle that makes much noise. Will you tell the others?" Mama John said.

The young boy, still speechless, nodded in agreement and then ran off.

Turning to her companion, Mama John sighed, "If they know I'm coming, then I see them carefully gathering the flock together at the unusual sound of my car."

"What happens if they don't know you?"

Again Mama John sighed and said, "Then they are afraid and their flocks scatter as they go running to hide. I try to meet as many as I can. I know that if any sheep are lost the boy faces severe punishment."

As time went by many of the children that she met waited eagerly for her arrival each week. They heard the sound of the motor and came to run beside the Land Rover. She arrived at the clinic to a crowd of laughing, clapping, and shouting children, "Mama John! Mama John!" What a welcome!

In her four-wheel drive Land Rover, Mama John carried all of the medical supplies and water she needed during her day's activities. The clinic was held in the small wooden building where Enkokidongoi Baptist Church had been meeting for several years.

The first day of the clinic everyone from the village came to see the event—both the sick and the well, the cows and the flies. Many bodies pressed closely together and all eyes watched through the doors, windows, and cracks in the wall as Mama John set up a room in the back of the church. Her clinic room consisted of a table and two chairs. Once she arranged her supplies, she was ready to go to work. She could not help being aware that her every move was closely scrutinized.

*It would not do to be self-conscious here*, she thought to herself as she felt the many eyes upon her.

One of her first patients was an elderly Maasai warrior. He was dressed in typical clothing for a Maasai. His only garment was a red cotton cloth tied over one shoulder and left to hang mid-thigh. Entering the room, he placed his spear beside the door. As he coughed, his slender chest heaved in obvious pain.

Mama John listened with her stethoscope. It was clear he had pneumonia and needed an antibiotic injection. Mama John prepared and injected it.

The medicine would not go in.

*The book never told us what to do when this happened,* she thought.

She tried again but finally accepted that she would have to remove the needle. She did so with great care and a great deal of difficulty.

"Whew," she whistled softly under her breath. "Would you look at that!"

The cause of the problem was evident. The man's skin was so tough that as the needle entered, it had actually made a U-turn.

Mama John looked at this toughened old warrior and wondered if he had a soft spot anywhere. After several more attempts, Mama John was finally able to give the man his injection. She marveled that as she treated this elderly man he showed no sign of pain or discomfort. Throughout the ordeal he remained expressionless. Only after completing the injection was Mama John rewarded with a toothless grin.

As the clinic continued, the number of patients increased as people came from farther away. Several of the men of Enkokidongoi Baptist Church offered to help Mama John. One of these men, named Wilson, began each Wednesday morning by reading out of the Bible in Kimaasai. Mama John did not speak Kimaasai and was thrilled to have someone read for her. She was thrilled, that is, until the day she glanced over Wilson's shoulder while he was reading only to discover that the Bible was upside down. What had Wilson been saying all this time?

Yet, in spite of his reading "skills," Wilson was a faithful helper. As a member of the Maasai tribe, his earlobes were pierced, stretched, and left to hang down on his shoulders in the customary manner.

One day Wilson was helping Mama John dress a wound. As he leaned forward to work, his earlobes swung forward in his way.

"Mama John," he called out, "can you help me?"

"Yes, what is it?" she asked.

"My ears . . ."

"Your ears?"

As Mama John glanced over she saw the problem. Quickly she reached around Wilson's head, twisted the lobes, and tucked them securely out of the way.

Wilson smiled his thanks.

As Mama John smiled back she realized just how much this man had come to trust her. She felt the harmony of kindred spirits as she looked at him working so hard to help her and to help this sick one. *So what if he can't read*, she thought.

The clinic days on the side of the mountain were always busy. Mama John worked as hard and as quickly as she could to see the many people that crowded around the church doors waiting to be seen. She often worked past dusk. To help her finish her work in the dark, Davis bought her a pressure lamp. One day while she was working, the lamp was stolen. As darkness came, Mama John kept working.

Missionary James Hampton was with her that day and he began to notice that it was getting too dark to work. But the sick still lined up before the clinic door, and Mama John continued to help them. Finally James said, "Mary, we've got to go."

"But James," she replied, "there are still sick people here that need to be seen. What would Jesus do?"

"Come on, Mary," he responded, "You ain't Jesus."

God's love in her was easy to see, and the Waarusha people came to love her deeply. One day during clinic some Waarusha women passed by on their way to a celebration. Their faces were painted white. Their heads, freshly shaven and oiled, glistened in the sunlight. Rows and rows of stiff, circular multicolored beads hung from their necks covering their breasts and reaching almost to their waists. The brass bracelets they wore jangled as they walked.

Colorful pieces of cloth called *kangas* were wrapped around their hips. They presented a picture of riotous color and indescribable beauty. They were happy that day, joyful of their beauty and the beauty of the world around them. It was a good day to sing and dance. They drew Mama John into their celebration as they brought her outside and began to sing and dance around her.

She saw humor in the situation and yet she could tell no one there because she knew they wouldn't understand. Here she was, Mary Hogg Saunders from Charleston, South Carolina, the only white face circled by a crowd of dancing Africans. She chuckled to herself and thought, *If they could see me now.*

In her mind she saw the big, black cauldron, bubbling and boiling in preparation for the next meal of boiled missionary. Any time now, Tarzan should come swinging in for an attempted rescue.

Mama John held her laughter until she got home that evening and shared the story with her family. But there, as she danced and clapped her hands, her greatest joy and the laughter she shared was that she had been included in their time of celebration.

As the people of Enkokidongoi learned more about Mama John, they began to notice that between Sunday School and worship she always slipped off into the cornfields right beside the church. This matter was brought before the church leaders, who decided it was not right that Mama John should have to do this. They knew that Western women were not accustomed to going to the bathroom in the cornfields.

A decision was made. Construction of an outdoor bathroom began. As the day of dedication drew near, many grew excited. They even obtained a commode seat. The structure was proudly constructed right by the church's front door.

The ceremonious day dawned and Mama John, as dignified as Queen Mary herself, stepped into the new bathroom. As she came out many clapped and cheered. Mama John's "john" had been christened![1]

Enkokidongoi Baptist Church continued to grow and young people came. Mama John saw a need for a youth Sunday School class and so she began to teach one. There were five young men in the class, but no girls with the exception of Niña, her daughter. Sunday School began each week with quoting the Scripture memory verse for that week. This was required, not optional, even for Niña. At the end of one year, everyone in her class received their own Bible as a gift from the church and as an encouragement for learning God's Word. It was the first book of any kind that the five young men had ever owned.

These five young men became known as Mama John's boys. Quietly she and Davis paid school fees for each of these young men, enabling them to obtain an education. They also bought each boy a school uniform every year so that they had the required attire for the government school they attended.

The first Sunday after they received their school uniforms, one of the five, Singa, came to church with his shoes on, carrying the shoelaces in his hand. He had not learned to tie a bow, having never owned a pair of shoes before. Davis was at Enkokidongoi that day and so together, he and Singa squatted in the dust of the church floor and Singa, as a teenager, practiced tying his first bow.

Each Saturday Mama John had jobs for these young men to do, either around the house or on the seminary campus. They learned much from her. How could they know that in the future Zephaniah would work for a bank, Sirikwa would lead the choir at Enkokidongoi Baptist Church, and Marko would go on with his education and work as a health official in the area. Singa, in just a few short years, would go to spend eternity with the Jesus, Whom he first met in the life of Mama John. He shared this same Jesus with his brother, John Kaipuko, who later became the pastor of Enkokidongoi Baptist Church.

As Mama John's nursing skills became known, Dr. Strausneider, a German doctor in Arusha, came to her with a request for help. He needed an extra assistant on the days he performed surgery. He had one regular assistant, a Maasai woman whom he had trained himself.

Soon after she agreed to help, Mama John was called out of a church service one Sunday morning to go into Arusha and assist with an emergency cesarean section. When she arrived at his clinic, the doctor had already scrubbed and was putting on his gown. Mama John began to scrub and as she did, she viewed the scene. Here was a physician speaking half German and half English, an American nurse answering in English or Swahili, and an African assistant responding only in Kimaasai. The woman on the operating table was an Asian who spoke Gujarati. Once again Mama John was amazed at the power of nonverbal communication. And the nonverbal communication was to continue, for in the following months another doctor arrived in Arusha to join the practice; he was Greek!

At the seminary a policy was established that students could not come unless they brought their wives. Often these men had accepted Christ as adults, coming from backgrounds where they were the only Christians in their families. Their wives did not yet know the Lord and, as one of their teachers, one of Mama John's responsibilities was to be a part of their learning more about Christ.

"Teach me to pray, Mama John," asked Gracie Wanje, one of her students.

They sat together after a seminary chapel service one morning.

Mama John began, "In the Bible we are given an example from the Psalms. Like David of many years ago, you and I can ask God to create a clean heart in us, and renew a right spirit within us in order that our hearts might be ready for prayer."

They spoke together for a few more minutes and then the two women bowed their heads in prayer.

"God," began Gracie, "Get a broom, and sweep out my heart. Sweep it good so that you get every corner. Then I can be clean."

"Amen," whispered Mama John.

"Amen."

Gracie had learned the meaning of the Scripture, and had applied it in her own words. To her, sweeping meant using a hand-made broom: a collection of hardy straw and thin sticks, bound together with a piece of string. With repetition, her broom could reach even the smallest piece of trash tucked away in the corners of her house. She wanted her heart that clean!

The pastors' wives classroom became a witnessing experience and many of the women came to accept Christ as their Savior. The church on campus was called N'garemtoni Baptist Church. The pastor at this time was Peter Kimiti, a friend of Mary and Davis from Nairobi, Kenya. It was Peter's privilege to baptize and disciple many of these new Christians as they came to join a church for the first time.

As a natural outgrowth of their experience, these women began to learn about sharing their faith. Each week Gladys Kimiti, the seminary wives, and Mama John would go into the town's marketplace.

In the market, stalls were lined up row after row with the goods placed on boxes, poles, grass mats, or plastic sheets. Goats, chickens, ducks, fruits, vegetables, baskets, spices, dresses, shirts, and even underwear were paraded for all to see. When bras were first sold, the women wore them at their waists, using the cups for two "side pockets." These pockets were especially useful for holding yarn and keeping the unused skein clean as the women knitted. Yes, the market was a place where things were happening.

After arriving at the market, the women gathered as a group. Mama John set up her pump organ and played and sang. She was careful when she invited people to come hear her *kinanda* (piano), remembering how embarrassed she had been when she had invited them all to her *kitanda* (bed) by mistake.

As people stopped to listen to the music, the women shared their faith. Mama John found great joy in these afternoons of singing hymns in Swahili in the market. But things did not always go smoothly, nor was it always easy.

The people of the market always found a chair for Mama John to sit on, and usually she was the only one sitting as she pumped air into the organ bellows with her legs moving in time to the music.

The Maasai men were always fascinated with this instrument and how it worked. Once when Davis visited the market, he heard Mama John's voice getting louder and louder. Walking over to the group he could not help but chuckle. There was his wife surrounded by a group of Maasai men, dressed traditionally in their one-robe garb. As they leaned closer and closer, they revealed more and more. Mama John's chair was at the wrong level. The closer they got, the more they showed, the louder she sang. By the time the hymn was over, the pace was a breakneck speed with everyone out of breath— Mama John included!

For many years her favorite hymn was *"Yesu Kwetu Ni Rafiki"* ("What a Friend We Have in Jesus"), and it became her trademark. Her daughter Lee teased her that the real reason she enjoyed singing in the market was that she had finally found a group of people who liked her singing.

Mama John's message of Christ's love was for all, to the ends of the earth. One day she felt as though she had gone just that far. She drove the car for several miles off of the dirt path known as the road, bumping through old cornfields and cabbage patches. Finally she reached a point where she could travel no further by car. Parking the car, she walked two more miles on a narrow footpath. She wrote to Davis's parents, describing the situation and her feelings:

"I went to visit a young girl who came to church last Sunday and said she wanted to know more about Jesus Christ. As I sat there with the young girl, her mother and two other women joined us. It was hard to look around and remember that this is the twentieth century. They did bring out one low stool and insisted I sit on it. All others sat on the ground. Always, even in this, it thrills me to tell again the wonderful story of love."

Mama John was very busy during the four years in Arusha, but not too busy to miss her three oldest children. This was the first term of service that boarding school was necessary. Lee, 13, Danner, 11, and John, 9, attended a school for missionary children in Kenya called Rift Valley Academy. Saying good-bye was not easy and many tears were shed as she and Davis drove back to Arusha after leaving three of their children behind. In the months and years that followed, Mama John was always writing a letter or baking some goodies to send to her children. She missed them terribly, and in one letter she wrote of her feelings to her family in the US.

*September 27, 1964*

*My dear folk,*

*I have just finished a letter to Lee, Danner, and John and I felt I wanted to write to you and say that this experience has made me love and appreciate you more than I ever knew before. These weeks have been far worse than I ever dreamed they would be. The hurt is so deep and just lingers. Surely it gets better as time goes by. I've missed them, oh, how I've missed them.*

*Let me share a few lines from some of their letters and you'll see how happy they are and how well they have settled in:*

*"The night I got the most homesick the dorm parent prayed with me. Today I'm much better. I like it here even though I miss you. I am on the 'tichy' basketball team."—John*

*"I like it here but I miss you. My roommate is so understanding. At night she lets me cry and talk. She's helped me so much. So far I've gotten all A's. I see John every day and we talk together about you and home. We just love our new school."—Danner*

*"Today I did 41 situps and threw the ball 96 yards. I see John every day and spend time with him. I am settled in and having a good time. You'll never know how comforting it is to read my Bible and pray when it gets really bad."—Lee*

*They have been just wonderful about writing. That, plus the fact that school here is in full swing, has helped some.*

*My love to you all and forgive me for not letting you know more often how much we do love you.*

*Mary*

Niña, the youngest was still at home. Without her brother and sisters she often got lonely. Since early childhood her one dream had been to own a horse. As she roamed the hills near the seminary campus one day she saw her chance. An old man was leading an animal that, in her seven-year-old eyes, was almost a horse. It was a donkey. She had saved her allowance and had five shillings (about 75 cents). She offered her money and struck a deal with the man. Proudly she came home leading her new purchase. Mama John looked out the kitchen window in time to see her daughter leading the filthiest, most flea-bitten, sway-backed mule she had ever seen. "Oh Davis . . ." she called.

Together they looked at the mule.

*It looks worse close up than it did from a distance,* groaned Mama John inwardly. There was no way they could keep this disease-ridden animal. She shared her thoughts.

"We have to return this mule to his home," agreed Davis.

Niña was crestfallen, but she understood, and told them where she had obtained her latest possession.

The mule was not nearly so cooperative. Davis pulled at the rope attached to its neck. It had no desire to move. Progress was slow, and only with a lot of pushing and prodding was this "almost horse" returned to its former owner. For a second time that day there was an exchange of money for mule.

Mama John comforted Niña by reminding her of her dogs, cats, rabbits, guinea pigs, and white mice.

"And just imagine, I thought that Lavelle Seats's pets were unusual when we were seminary students in Kentucky!" Mama John said to Davis with a smile.

Within a woman's life are markers that note the passage of time. They include the lines that crease eyes, those little aches and pains in the early morning and late night, and the arrival of white hair. For Mama John, the arrival of those white strands came early. She was not yet ready to be white-haired, so she purchased a bottle of brown hair dye.

Returning home, she went to work. The results were disastrous! Her hair turned a brassy yellow-orange-gold.

*Another try,* she thought, *This has got to be better. It just can't get any worse.*

She applied the dye and waited. After the correct amount of time, she shampooed as directed.

"Oh no!" She couldn't believe her eyes.

Her hair was now a bile-green. It made her sick just looking at it.

"I've done enough," she declared. "It's time for some help."

She made arrangements with Feeza, a local hairdresser in Arusha, to help her with her problem. First, a severe haircut was performed to get rid of most of her curly green cap. Then, after several weeks of allowing her hair to "rest" from its trauma, another dye was applied.

"I can't believe it!" Mama John exclaimed.

Feeza began to apologize, "I don't know what happened . . ."

Together they looked at her hair, which now had a bluish-purple tint.

"Well," conceded Mama John, "I've learned one thing from all of this. White hair sounds just FINE to me."

And from that day on, Mama John allowed her hair to turn white naturally.

Other markers in the passage of time for Mama John were the days when her children came home from boarding school. Vacation time from school was a happy time. The family did things together, though perhaps not typical things.

One year Arusha was plagued with a smallpox epidemic. It was essential that as many as possible be vaccinated quickly. Mama John and her children all went to work assembly-line style. John's job was to write names; Danner swabbed arms with alcohol; Lee prepared the medication; Mama John gave the vaccinations; and Niña handed out the candy after the ordeal was over. Davis was the general superintendent of the entire project.

Vacation time also meant good food. How Mama John could cook! The family sat down in the evenings to meals such as artichoke hearts for appetizers and a main course of gazelle steaks, scalloped potatoes, glazed carrots, and homemade rolls. Desserts were always delicious. With a beautiful table set with fresh roses from the garden as the centerpiece, Mama John had a specific purpose in mind. She always said that even though her children were growing up in the heart of Africa, they would grow up being able to sit at the tables of princes or paupers and feel just as comfortable with either.

Mama John's cooking was superb. For those who tasted her rolls it was easy to understand why it was almost impossible to turn one —or even a second one—away because of their "melt in your mouth" quality. Below is her recipe.

## MAMA JOHN'S ROLLS

Mix 2 tablespoons of yeast in 1/2 cup of lukewarm water. Add 1 teaspoon of sugar. Stir and set aside.

In a large mixing bowl, cream together 1/2 cup of margarine and 1/2 cup of sugar. Add 1 teaspoon of salt.

Add 2 eggs, one at a time, mixing well.

Set aside 2 cups of lukewarm water and 6 cups of flour.

Combine and mix well all of the above ingredients, alternating dry and liquid until the dough is of the same consistency. It will be sticky.

Brush with oil and let rise for a few hours. (It's easier to handle if refrigerated for this period of time.)

Punch down, place on a floured board, knead briefly, and shape into knots, buns, or rolls. Allow dough to rise again. Bake at 350°F for 10 to 15 minutes, until light brown.

Serve with love.

For many, holiday time becomes sadly nostalgic if one is separated from family. Yet, the bonds of love between the missionaries in Tanzania became the ties of family. Children called their parent's co-workers *aunt* and *uncle* and there was a sense of being a part of the family of God.

Thus, Christmas continued as a *family* time with traditions and laughter. One such tradition during the years in Arusha was the tradition of the *long johns*. Once, a bright red pair of long johns was sent, as requested, for someone who was going to climb Mount Kilimanjaro. The climbing experience was long over, but the long-john experience lived on.

Each year, as names were chosen for the sharing of gifts, all knew that someone would receive "the gift!" A part of "the gift" was not only obtaining the use of the long johns for a year, but also modeling the gift on that day for all to enjoy. What laughter filled the room.

"Can you hear them laughing still?" asked one of the kids.

"Yeah, our parents are really hooting. But we've already seen Uncle James in the long johns; what else could be *that* funny?"

"Let's go see."

As the kids peeked around the doorway they were amazed at what they saw. They didn't know it was a game called *Ha Ha*. All they knew was that each of the ten parents were lying on the floor with their heads on someone else's stomach. In order to fit everyone in the room, the adults were configured much like an interwoven crossword puzzle.

"Begin the game again," called out Uncle Earl.

"Ha," laughed his wife. Just one ha, and her stomach lifted her husband's head, which was placed on her abdomen.

"Ha, Ha," he followed, and the head on his stomach lifted two times.

"Ha, Ha, Ha," was the next line, by the third person. By then, all were laughing, and the harder they laughed the more their heads bounced on each other's stomachs.

"Our parents are crazy," agreed all the kids as they went back to their own Christmas games.

The four years in Arusha were happy, fruitful years. As the Saunderses left for furlough in 1968, Mama John's one sorrow was that there was no nurse to carry on her clinic work among the Waarusha people. The area, which had been so unresponsive to learning about Christ, now had a strong church with a pastor.

As she was preparing to leave, the people of Enkokidongoi helped her prepare for her travels by giving her a large drinking gourd as a farewell gift. For them, to travel without a container for water was unthinkable. They decorated the dried container with colorful beads and then went to the market and paid someone to scratch the words "Mama John" on the bottom. Their gift was presented amidst tears of farewell and for many years after, when a

1968: The faculty of the Baptist Theological Seminary of East Africa in Arusha, Tanzania. Top row, l to r: Jack Partain, James Hampton, Tom McMillan, Davis Saunders; bottom row, l to r: Ruth Partain, Gena Hampton, Mary "Mama John" Saunders, Marilyn McMillan.

Land Rover drove on the sides of Mount Meru, the people remembered and the children ran, calling, "Mama John, Mama John."

[1]Mama John's john remains to this day.

# LIMURU, KENYA

*"And the King will answer and say to them,*
*'Truly I say to you, to the extent that you did it to one*
*of these brothers of Mine, even the least*
*of them, you did it to Me'"*

(Matt. 25:40).

In 1969 Davis was asked to become the field representative for eastern Africa. Returning from furlough meant a move to Limuru, a small community just outside of Nairobi, Kenya. Here, Davis became more involved in administration with his fellow missionaries throughout the East African countries. Once more Mama John began to pray about her role as they settled into this familiar, yet rapidly changing area.

One day Bwana Daniel Mathuku, Mama John's old friend from Shauri Moya, took Mama John on a trip toward Nairobi. Along the way they stopped to rest.

"Let's get out of the car," suggested Bwana Daniel.

Mama John did as the tall, husky pastor suggested.

"What is there to see here?" Mama John wondered aloud.

"If you will walk with me to the edge of the road you will see what I have seen," replied Bwana Daniel. He motioned for her to follow.

At the edge of the road the ground rapidly dropped off and Mama John saw for the first time a place called Mathari Valley. The valley was approximately seven miles long and a half mile wide. An entire community had sprung up rapidly in the valley as an overflow from Nairobi. As was happening in many parts of Africa, people, young people in particular, were attracted to the lure of big-city life and were moving from the rural areas to the cities. Many came seeking a new life, but jobs were scarce and few had any education or job training.

The scene before Mama John was indescribable. Thousands lived in shanties made of scraps of cardboard and corrugated iron. No signs of sanitation were visible, but infection and disease were easily visible. In Mama John's experienced eyes she saw needs and knew that she must help.

"All right, Bwana Daniel," she replied, "I have seen with my eyes and with my heart. What do we do next?"

"The problem will be getting a permit to open a clinic. I have asked and have been told that the Nairobi city government does not recognize that this community exists. It will be very difficult to get a permit to work here," Bwana Daniel answered.

"So what can we do?"

"Pray. We must pray that God will help us find a way."

After much prayer and thought Mama John began by opening a baby clinic. Obtaining a permit took a long time, but permission was finally obtained.

The city council gave Mama John a small room in which to hold a clinic, but it soon proved inadequate.

*Where can the money be found to build and maintain a bigger clinic?* Mama John wondered.

Volunteers offered their assistance. Barbara Cunningham and John Adams, fellow missionaries, offered to help. Together they committed to pray for the Mathari Valley Clinic.

"John," Mama John asked one day, "How much would it take to build a small clinic here?"

"I'd say you need about $400," he replied.

And so they prayed specifically, humbly, and consistently, "Lord, we need $400 to begin a clinic here."

Back in Florida, a Christian woman had been blessed with a bumper crop of oranges that year. She felt led to give an extra portion of her profits to missions work.

A letter from the United States arrived one day that sent Mama John hurrying to find Bwana Daniel.

"Bwana Daniel, Bwana Daniel, you'll never believe what just arrived!" she exclaimed, excited.

"You have $400?" Bwana Daniel asked.

"No, not $400. A woman in Florida was blessed with a successful orange crop this year, and she wants to share with others her blessing. She was a visitor here in Kenya last year, and she saw Mathari Valley. After returning home she felt a burden for this place. She set aside $400 to send to us, but she also told other women in her church about Mathari Valley. These other women want to help as well."

Mama John paused for a moment.

"The check they sent isn't for $400, it is for $1,400!" Mama John exclaimed.

*Bwana asifiwe* (Praise the Lord) was all Bwana Daniel could say.

Construction for a new building quickly got underway. Meanwhile, the clinic continued in the assigned room. More volunteers came to help.

One such helper introduced herself to Mama John.

"I am the second wife to Joshua," the young woman began. "His first wife is Gloria."

Mama John thought back to the conversation she had so many years ago with Gloria, and looked in amazement at this young woman.

"How is Gloria?" Mama John asked. Many years had passed since they had seen one another.

"Gloria is well," the woman answered. "She has asked me to give you her greetings. I also want to tell you that knowing her has changed my life. She has told me about Jesus, and I, too, am a Christian."

With joy Mama John realized that Gloria had looked beyond her own circumstances and shared God's love with this beautiful young woman.

The clinic stayed busy.

Mothers came early on clinic days to line up outside. Volunteers helped to count pills and distribute powdered milk.

Week after week, however, Mama John noticed babies that did not return. She wrote one sentence across their file card: Death due to malnutrition. Repeatedly she told the mothers, "If you could just feed them a handful of crushed peanuts or mashed beans each day, they might live."

"But where do we get the peanuts?" mothers asked in response. "How can we find the beans?" Their own breast milk had long since dried up.

It was heartbreaking. For the first time in her career Mama John witnessed widespread malnutrition. These women had nothing. They had left their families and their village farms to seek work. Now they found themselves stranded in this metropolitan desert. The clinic was an oasis.

Other clinic volunteers met outside to talk and visit with patients waiting to be seen. Women's groups from nearby churches assisted. Nell Woodard, an American whose husband had come to Kenya to work in aviation, learned of the need and came. Milton Cunningham brought tape recorders with tapes teaching about Christ. Persons waiting outside could sit in small groups around the recorder and listen. Opportunities to share hope in Christ were endless.

The work continued and God blessed it. Amazingly, there was always just enough money to buy the necessary supplies of medicine and powdered milk. Often Mama John would hand out the final bag of powdered milk to the last mother and baby who had waited all day for help.

Help came from unexpected sources.

"Here is a check for $500," said Barbara Cunningham one morning as she handed Mama John an envelope. "It's from Mr. Broyhill."

"Mr. Broyhill of Broyhill furniture?" Mama John asked in disbelief.

"Yes," said Barbara, smiling.

"I don't think I've ever met him."

"You haven't," replied Barbara, "but he was visiting and learned about the clinic. He sent this money to be used as needed."

The clinic continued to grow, and eventually a new clinic building replaced the weather-beaten room. In time, on Sundays, a church was started using that same room.

When it was time for Mama John to return to the States a missionary nurse, Nancy Jones, stood ready to continue the work. In all her years of nursing this was the only time another nurse was ready to continue the work Mama John had been doing.

As field representative, Davis traveled frequently to the countries of Eastern and Southern Africa. Knowing he would be gone a great deal, Davis purchased a Volkswagen car so that his wife could travel about as needed. The old, blue, bug was nicknamed *Mathari*.

Sunday mornings found Mama John driving Mathari into Nairobi to attend church at Shauri Moya. In Swahili *shauri moya* means *affairs of the heart*. How true this was for Mama John. Bwana Daniel was pastor of the church. Elizabeth Wanjiru, her best friend and one who had helped from the beginning, was leader of women's work there. Mama John taught a Sunday School class. She was now fluent in Swahili, but Elizabeth continued to tease her. *Umejaribu* (you have tried), Elizabeth would say to her. Together they would laugh and remember Mama John's early attempts at language learning. Then, *umejaribu* was all Elizabeth would say, for fear of hurting Mama John's feelings, knowing her Swahili was incorrect.

Attending Shauri Moya was an affair of Mama John's heart. How she loved this area and these people. Years later, this church honored Mary and Davis with a retirement service. After showering them with gifts, they were asked to stand at the front of the church. Persons who had accepted Christ 35 years earlier through the lives and ministry of the Saunderses were invited to come forward and stand beside them. Next, those who had been taught by these first Christians joined them. Then, those who had accepted Christ through the second generation of believers joined their teachers and role models. The process continued until Davis and Mama John were surrounded by three generations of Christians.

"You see here," spoke the pastor that day, "the results of faithful servants who planted a seed. Today, as we honor them, they can now see the fruit from the seeds planted so many years ago."

Tragedy also followed on the missions field. While living in Limuru, Mama John received the tragic news that her youngest brother, Johnny, and his wife had been killed in a collision with a drunken, teenage driver. They left behind four children. Jeff, the youngest, was sitting in between his parents and sustained severe damage to his legs. Doctors were concerned he would never walk again.

"How can I help from way over here?" Mama John asked Davis when she heard the news. "I feel helpless. Why, I hardly even know the children. It's been years since we saw them. Still, I know I should help. What can we do?"

Unknown to Mama John, plans were already underway. The people of Citadel Square Baptist Church in Charleston, South Carolina, knew of the situation. In no time funds were sent to enable Mama John to fly back to the States. She went not knowing what to expect.

Arriving in Charleston, she was greeted by family and friends.

She stayed at her parents' home. Her mother was glad to see her and welcomed her warmly. Mama John was shocked and saddened to see how poor her father's health had become. She knew he had been diagnosed with cancer, but his weakened condition still jarred her emotionally. Family members there had seen him on a daily basis. Not having seen him for some time, Mama John had to experience stages of grief that others in the family had already passed through.

She gathered herself together. She knew she must be prepared to meet with her niece and nephews.

There was a knock on the door.

"Come in," called Mama John.

Hearing a sigh, she looked up to see a small, pixie-faced girl peeking around the door.

"Hello, Cathy," she said gently. "Do come in."

To Cathy, Mama John was a stranger, a woman who had come from far away.

To Mama John, Cathy was a precious, dark-haired ten-year-old in a miniskirt and boots. Cathy was also timid and shy, and obviously overwhelmed by the situation.

As she looked at the trembling young girl, Mama John knew what she must do.

The three boys, aged 14, 13, and 6, followed Cathy into the room. Mama John spoke with all four, offering to adopt them. Jeff, the youngest, and Cathy were willing to go to Africa, but the two older boys, already teenagers, preferred staying in the United States.

Mama John called back to East Africa that night.

"Davis? How do you feel about having two more kids?"

"I'll rely on your judgment," was his response.

And so the Saunders family grew from six to eight.

The time in the United States was not easy. Mama John was exhausted helping care for Jeff, who still needed constant care; preparing two children for international travel; and finalizing legal arrangements to become the children's mother. She knew she was close to the limit of what she could handle.

Yet, another sorrow was to come. Her father's condition began to deteriorate rapidly. The week she was to return to East Africa, he passed away.

When asked what she planned to do, she said, "I will fulfill a promise I made to my father."

"What promise was that?" asked a friend.

"He asked that I sing at his funeral," she replied. "I can hear him now with his Southern drawl, 'Meery, I like to hear you sing, girl.'"

She was so glad that her father had come to know the Savior as his own. The day of the funeral, inner strength from her heavenly Father was evident as she stood beside his grave and sang:

*There is a place of quiet rest,*
*Near to the heart of God,*
*A place where sin cannot molest,*
*Near to the heart of God.*

*There is a place of comfort sweet,*
*Near to the heart of God,*
*A place where we our Savior meet,*
*Near to the heart of God.*

*There is a place of full release,*
*Near to the heart of God,*
*A place where all is joy and peace,*
*Near to the heart of God.*

*O Jesus, blest Redeemer,*
*Sent from the heart of God,*
*Hold us who wait before thee*
*Near to the heart of God.*

The next week Mama John returned to Limuru with Jeff and Cathy. Jeff was still unable to walk or take care of himself in any way. Cathy was coming to terms with a world where everything familiar was gone. To her, Mama John's world was a different planet.

As the three debarked the plane in Kenya, Mama John held tightly to Cathy's hand while carrying Jeff. The familiar form of Davis came into view. Mama John began to cry the tears she had held back for weeks. "Oh, Davis, I sure have missed you."

His 6 foot 3 inch-solid frame held her as she leaned up against him. His rough, calloused hands patted her lovingly as he sought to lift some of her burden. They were a team; they needed each other.

Having two new children in the home brought new experiences to the Saunders family. In the early 1970s the Mau Mau attempted a revival in Kenya. Tensions mounted as threats were made. Davis hated that he had to travel so much, leaving Mama John alone with the children. As one of several security precautions, a siren was placed on the roof of their house, connected to the local police station. Its use had never been tested. One night Mama John and Davis awakened to find Cathy in their bedroom.

"Mama John," whispered Cathy, "I'm having a bad dream. Can I get in bed with you?" The two adults scooted to one side to make room for the little girl.

Before settling down Cathy requested, "Can I turn on a light, just for a minute?"

She reached over in the dark and flipped a switch. No lights came on. Instead, a siren began to sound. Loud and piercing, it left no one in the neighborhood asleep.

Cathy had missed the light switch and set off the alarm instead. Davis quickly rolled over and turned it off.

Within minutes a Tigoni police car pulled in the driveway. All were impressed by their response, except, of course, the police. To them a young girl setting off an alarm was a serious matter. How could they understand the difficulties of a child adapting to a new culture?

Adjustments were needed on everyone's part. Jeff, in particular, grew tired of waiting for someone to carry him around. He began to pull himself with his arms while sitting down and dragging his feet behind. Slowly but surely, this determined freckle-faced, red-headed boy began to try and walk.

"Mama John, Mama John!" he called out one day.

Not knowing what it could be, Mama John came running.

There stood Jeff. He pushed his chest out proudly and took a deep breath.

"Just watch me now!"

Slowly and carefully, Jeff took a step.

Step followed step, and before long Jeff was running around like the normal little boy he was.

Jeff loved to ask questions. A typical exchange might be, "What kind of trees are those you have growing in the butter?"

"That's called parsley, Jeff. It's for decoration."

One evening when the Saunders family was seated around the dinner table with guests, Jeff asked a question.

"Mama John, what's a louse?"

"Let's talk about that later," she responded quietly.

A few minutes passed. Then, "Well, my teacher said to ask you."

"Ask me what, Jeff?"

"To check whether or not I have a louse."

"All right, Jeff, we'll talk about it later."

A few more minutes passed.

"My friend Disho has lots of louses."

"That's lice," interjected Davis.

"We've been swapping hats, so we might have swapped lice, too."

With the meal already interrupted, Mama John headed upstairs with Jeff in tow. Sure enough, he had lice. Later that evening, she began the required shampoos to treat the problem.

"I've got the doughnuts ready," called Mama John, "and I'm

ready to go see John play rugby." She and Davis were preparing to visit three of their children at Rift Valley Academy (RVA).

Danner and John were still at boarding school at the Rift Valley Academy. Niña had joined them. Limuru was close enough for frequent visits, especially for sporting events. John was quite an athlete and the captain of the rugby team. Homemade doughnuts happened to be a favorite of all the Saunders children.

Davis looked in the back of the car. Dozens of freshly-made doughnuts were stacked on trays.

"I know you like to go to RVA, but I have a feeling the kids like you to come even more than you like to go," he remarked.

"You're probably right and I love it," replied Mama John. "Let's go or we'll be late for the game. Do you think the doughnuts have anything to do with me being called the team mascot?"

Davis chuckled. "Well, it's not because of your knowledge of the sport. The only time you holler is when John has the ball or is being tackled."

"That's right. I either yell, 'That's my boy,' or 'Get off my boy.'"

One evening Mama John and Davis went into Nairobi for dinner. As they walked down a street they heard a group playing a popular song. The music was coming from a sandwich shop.

As they neared the shop, Mama John asked, "Does that voice sound familiar to you?"

A sign outside boasted live entertainment. Looking inside, Mama John and Davis spotted their youngest daughter, Niña, singing and playing her guitar.

"Did you know she was going to be here?" asked Davis.

"I don't think so," said Mama John. "I'm as surprised as you are. Oh, Davis, it reminds me of just how much our children are growing up. They are all so independent."

"That was our aim, wasn't it?" Davis reminded her. "We wanted to encourage independence. It can't be easy for them to think of living in the United States without us. We have known this separation across continents would begin after high school, even though none of us have looked forward to it."

Upon returning to Kenya after a furlough, this new kind of separation occurred. Lee, a sophomore in college, stayed behind in the States. By the end of the tour in Limuru, both Danner and John joined their sister.

Those were not easy times. Living as a divided family was difficult. Mama John often felt helpless to support her children through difficult times they were experiencing. Telephone calls were inadequate and expensive. The children's roots were in East Africa, and adjusting to living in the United States was not easy. Such is the case of many missionaries' kids. They may look like Americans on the outside, but often their souls cry out for the homeland of their childhood.

When the time came for returning to the United States for another furlough, Mama John drove *Mathari* to Shauri Moya.

Bwana Daniel came out to greet her.

As she said farewell to him, she handed him the keys to the Volkswagen. "Mathari was given to me to get me where I needed to go, and I want to give it to you to help you get where you need to go," she said to him.

She hugged him good-bye. "I am sad to leave and yet filled with joy at the thought of our family being reunited again."

# CHAPTER 8

# RICHMOND, VIRGINIA

*"That I may know Him, and the power of His
resurrection and the fellowship of His sufferings, being
conformed to His death; . . . I press on toward the goal
for the prize of the upward call of God in Christ Jesus"*

*(Phil. 3:10,14).*

"Mary, it's official. I have been asked to become area director for Eastern and Southern Africa." Davis shared the news after hanging up the phone in their tiny furlough apartment.

"How do you feel about this?" she asked.

"To tell you the truth," replied Davis, "I would rather be in Ogbomosho, Nigeria, working as a bush missionary than to face what I know lies ahead as area director. But, putting aside how I feel, I believe that this job is what God would have me do."

"What will I do, Davis?"

"This will be hardest on you," he answered. "The Board recognizes my position, but you will no longer be called a missionary."

Mama John silently began processing the changes that lay before her. Another move would be made, but not back to beloved

Africa. Davis was moving into a position of great challenge, she recognized, but what would her challenge be? Her role was now to support her husband in his work. For the first time in 25 years, they would not work as a team, side by side. The thought was painful.

They made the decision as their furlough time in Louisville, Kentucky, came to a close in the spring of 1973. Once again, as he had in all previous furloughs, Davis attended Southern Seminary.

The seminary allowed them to live in campus housing. By now the Saunders family numbered seven. To create an apartment big enough, the seminary knocked down a wall between two apartments. Still, there were only three bedrooms. Jeff's bed was set up in the room with the washer and dryer. His clothes were folded next to detergents and cleaning products.

"Mama John," he asked when he saw where his room would be for the year, "does this mean that I sleep in the laundry room or do you do laundry in my bedroom?"

Everyone laughed! It was a time for flexibility in tight living conditions.

During this year Davis received his doctoral degree. After years of school during furlough, late nights in the library, and studying in the bathroom because it was the quietest room in the house, Davis became Dr. Saunders. As he went forward to receive his degree, Mama John stood proudly with the rest of the family, applauding him.

Several who worked with him asked, "What shall we call you now? Dr. Saunders?"

Mama John interjected, "I don't know what you will call him, but you can call me Mrs. Dr. Saunders."

After graduation the family moved to Richmond. At first Mama John could find no direct need for her talents, and the early months in Richmond were lonely. Her family was aware of her hurt, yet they felt hopeless to ease it. Mama John knew that God had guided the move to Richmond, yet the love of her life was her African family.

Not long after Davis began his new job he realized that his

knowledge of East and West Africa far outweighed that of Central and Southern Africa. A six-month stay was planned in Harare, Zimbabwe (then called Salisbury, Rhodesia), so that he could become better acquainted with the missionaries and the ministry among Christians in the southern part of Africa. Mama John was delighted.

After settling into a house in the modern city of Harare, Mama John began looking for opportunities to be involved with the people there. She was invited to work with the women in the churches. What fun she had singing and dancing with the women as they met, wearing their uniforms of blue skirts and purple tops.

The time in Zimbabwe flew by. Upon returning to Richmond, Mama John once again faced loneliness and discouragement. Seeking her own place of ministry, she took a job as a staff nurse in a local hospital. She worked full time in an effort to learn new nursing skills and update ones she had not used in her 25 years of clinical nursing in Africa.

"Where's mom?" asked Danner one evening after school.

"She's on the phone," came the reply.

"Do you know who she's talking to?"

"I think it's one of her patients."

Sure enough, Mama John sat in the den, talking to a patient. "I was just thinking about you today and wondering how you were feeling," Danner heard her ask.

Mama John's approach to nursing often amazed those she worked with, for she cared not only for the physical needs but also the spiritual needs of her patients and their families. At home it was not unusual to hear her talking to patients by phone just to see how they were doing or to hear her praying with family members during difficult moments. In Africa she had learned to minister to the whole person as she helped those with such tremendous needs there. These people were no different.

During this time Mama John's mother suffered a fall which resulted in a fractured hip. Her mother had been living independently in

Charleston, South Carolina, but Mama John felt she needed extra care until she recovered, so Grandmother Hogg came to live with the Saunders clan. At the same time, Jeff underwent major surgery on his legs, which left him immobilized in a body cast for months.

Mama John tried to maintain her full-time hospital nursing job as well as nurse the two patients at home. It wasn't easy. One morning after working the night shift, Mama John pulled up to a stoplight after exiting the freeway. The light was red, so she waited.

Tap, tap, tap. Tap, tap, tap.

*What was that noise?* she wondered.

Tap, tap, tap.

There it was again.

Mama John stirred and then realized she was sitting in her car. She looked around. Through her side window she encountered a set of very angry eyes.

"Lady, that light has changed two times already. You need to move your car."

Mama John looked sheepishly behind her. A row of cars waited, honking their horns impatiently. She had fallen asleep. The only thing that had kept her from rolling out into busy morning traffic was her foot on the brake.

"That's enough," said Davis when he heard what happened.

Something had to change. Mama John decided to quit her hospital job and return to working full time at home. It turned out to be a wise decision, for within a year all six children were living at home again. Four of the six were no longer children really, but young adults. Davis threatened to paint lines in the driveway and advertise as a used car lot. It wasn't a bad idea with six vehicles all lined up in a row each night.

Living together again proved to be a good time for the Saunders family to spend time together and renew close-knit ties. It was not unusual for them to spend an evening much like they had in East Africa where they would pull out guitars and sing many of the old ballads they had grown up hearing. Little did they know that in the

years ahead, times like these would be few. Continents would separate them as God called each to different places of service.

Within the same year, Grandmother Hogg died. Mama John
was grateful that in her mother's last years she had been able to care
for her. They had lived through so many years of separation. Still, it
was a difficult time.

Just as she had for her father, Mama John sang at her mother's
service. Her voice trembled as she stood beside her mother's grave
to sing once again:

*O Jesus, blest Redeemer,*
*Sent from the heart of God,*
*Hold us who wait before thee*
*Near to the heart of God.*

Mama John continued searching for new ways to share her gifts
in ministry. Public speaking had always been one of her gifts. She
enjoyed sharing, and found herself speaking and teaching often.

One evening she was invited to speak about East Africa at a
church. She prepared herself thoroughly, even going so far as to
wear East African dress. That night she wore a blouse and wrap-
around cloth called a *kanga,* just as many women in East Africa
wear. As she spoke that night, however, she noticed people were not
looking at her but rather down in their laps. Finally, one member of the
congregation lifted her hand.

Mama John acknowledged her. "Is there something you need to
say?" she asked.

"I thought you'd like to know that your piece of material is on
the floor," said the woman, embarrassed.

Mama John looked down. In her moving about and talking,
her kanga had come unwrapped. She found herself standing in
front of 50 people in a blouse and slip! Unabashed, she picked up
the colorful piece of material and said, "I know each of you has
wondered how to put one of these things on. At this time I'd like to

demonstrate for you." Demonstration over, she picked up where she had stopped and continued speaking.

One day Mama John came home to find a surprise. Davis had bought her a beautiful piano as a love gift. Immediately she sat down and began to play and sing *"Yesu Kwetu Ni Rafiki"* ("What a Friend We Have in Jesus"). Her love for her Best Friend, Jesus, had never wavered. Listening to her play, her family could picture her pumping that old pump organ in Arusha, gathering together the people of the marketplace and sharing out of the depth of her heart the message she had for the world.

During the summer of 1979 Mama John became aware of the need for relief work in the country of Uganda. A devastated people group had been left behind after the ravaging hand of Ugandan leader Idi Amin had swept the country. Missionaries in Uganda had requested volunteer help and were delighted to learn that Mama John was on her way.

When she arrived in the town of Jinja, Uganda, the country was still not safe and a night curfew was imposed on all. Many armed soldiers roamed about. Missionaries Jim and Linda Rice often dropped Mama John and her boxes of medicine at a church in the morning and returned to collect her in the evening. She worked tirelessly, to the point that it became increasingly difficult to get her to stop seeing patients. She thrived on her contact with those in need, ignoring her own needs. Often the missionaries threatened to have two husky guys pack her up with her boxes and bring her in each night.

After several months in Uganda, Mama John returned to the US. Once again she faced discouragement and felt out of place. Often she was lonely. For months she carried her Swahili Bible to church, translating in her mind the sermons into Swahili. She was so sure that the Lord would not leave her in America and that one day she would need to use her Swahili again.

Finally, in despair, she called out to God.

"Why God? Why Richmond?" she cried, falling down on her knees. As her tears fell, she waited.

Then, in her heart she heard the answer from her Father.

"Mary, you can go back to Africa any time you want to. You can go with your fellow missionaries and your African friends."

"How, Lord?"

"As you pray."

Falling down on her face, she begged, "Lord, teach me to pray."

Then she thought of another Mary, a Mary of long ago—the mother of Jesus. How difficult it must have been for that girl; how lonely and discouraging. Yet, her response had been, "My soul exalts the Lord, And my spirit has rejoiced in God my Savior. For He has had regard for the humble state of His bondslave; . . . For the Mighty One has done great things for me; And holy is His name" (Luke 1:46-48a,49).

The request burned within her.

"Lord, teach me to pray."

As she waited, the answer came from the Word of God. "I waited patiently for the Lord; And He inclined to me, and heard my cry. He brought me up out of the pit of destruction, out of the miry clay; And He set my feet upon a rock making my footsteps firm. And He put a new song in my mouth, a song of praise to our God" (Psalm 40:1-3a).

"Lord, teach me to pray," she continued.

Again the answer came. "As the deer pants for the water brooks, So my soul pants for Thee, O God. My soul thirsts for God, for the living God; . . . Why are you in despair, O my soul? And why have you become disturbed within me? Hope in God, for I shall again praise Him For the help of His presence" (Psalm 42:1-2a,5).

Throughout her years of service, Mama John had felt that she knew how to pray. Prayer had been a part of her daily life. Yet from this time on, Mama John's prayer life developed as it never had before. It became a source of strength such as she had never experienced. Her relationship with her Heavenly Father took on new and wonderful insights. Prayer became the focus of her ministry. Her gift of intercessory prayer became her avenue of involvement in Davis's work and in missions. She spent hours in intercession for missionaries and their needs. She went to Africa daily on her knees.

As she was praying one day, the phone rang.

"Hello," Mama John answered.

A voice with a decidedly African accent spoke, "This is the international operator with a call from Kenya. Is this 320-3015?"

"Yes, it is," answered Mama John, excited.

"Go ahead, your call is through."

"Mama John, I am calling to ask you to pray for me."

And so, through her prayers, she remained involved in Africa. Yet, deep down she knew that her service with her African brothers and sisters was not yet finished. Another chapter of her life remained to be written. God, the Author of her life, had yet to tell her of Ethiopia.

# RABEL, ETHIOPIA

*"And my God shall supply all your needs according
to His riches in glory in Christ Jesus"*

*(Phil. 4:19).*

T he sound of the alarm clock awoke her, 3:30 A.M. This was the
time to spend in prayer before the truck was ready to go. As
she prayed, Mama John again felt God's presence. In this presence
she waited quietly, asking for His strength, His peace, His love to
fill her.

A short while later, a voice called out. "Ready?" asked missionary veterinarian, Jerry Bedsole.

She was, wasn't she?

Little did Mama John know that the next four months would
touch her life and change her in a way nothing ever had before. That
morning before leaving, she passed a few quickly written letters to
Rosie, Jerry's wife, asking her to mail them for her.

*March 15, 1985*

*Dear family,*

*I am in Addis Ababa today and will be on my way to the Menz-Gishe area at 4:45 A.M. These last couple of days have been so busy with more and more details. Today I finally got a security clearance for two months. I may have to return to Addis later and go through this all over again.*

*We have received reports that hundreds and hundreds are migrating to the Menz-Gishe area because food and drugs are there. More drugs are loaded on the truck that we will take tomorrow. Today we bought some dry soup mix and tea. We plan to eat with the Ethiopians but because it is so cold, soup will taste good. I'm told that there is no way I can imagine just what I will experience these next few months. The name of the village we will be staying in is called Rabel. I'm still quite sure that I'm where the Father wants me to be and I'm quite ready to leave Addis. God has been so wonderful with His promises and assurances. With all my heart I give thanks for this opportunity.*

*Please share with those at church that I'm counting on their prayers.*

Rabel, Ethiopia: Mama Jolui and her assistants dress the wounds of a child who fell into a cooking fire.

*I know the resources that are mine, but I also know the power of prayer. I'll write again, but I wanted you to know that you are in my thoughts and prayers even as I begin this adventure of living in Rabel with God.*

*How I love you,*
*Mama John*

The truck bumped up and down, straining to continue on its arduous trip. Part of the road had been carved out of the sides of canyons with hand tools: carved by Ethiopian men using what little strength they had to prepare a way for the relief they needed so desperately; carved by men who were proud, hardworking, independent; carved and leveled rock by rock! The view was spectacular: gigantic canyons of varying colors of red and brown diving deeply to dry riverbeds and racked, course clay.

Finally they arrived in Rabel, the capital city of the Menz-Gishe province. Looking at the dry, barren land, it was difficult to believe that in the Amharic language the meaning of *Rabel* was *city without hunger.* For its 30,000 inhabitants, nothing could be further from the truth. The trees were all gone and the streets were parched and cracked beyond any semblance of the earth that had once covered the winding streets of this tiny town.

As Mama John moved through the town, she was struck by the intense sorrow in the faces of the people she saw. Around many of their necks hung the Coptic cross, a sign of faith in the Ethiopian Orthodox Church which, until 1976, had been Ethiopia's official state religion. Historically the Ethiopian Orthodox Church had been a political institution, playing a significant role in unifying Ethiopians with a common faith. About 20,000 churches and monasteries were scattered across the country, and services were still conducted in Geez, an ancient language used only for religious purposes and understood by very few.

However, in the early 1980s a bloody civil war had raged as a Marxist government took control. Now, major political changes were sweeping the country. To compound the problems, by early

1985 a famine of unforeseen proportions had taken 300,000 lives. Mama John knew all this. She knew there was much to do. The physical needs of these people were an obvious priority.

Mama John learned that the closest water source was at least an hour's walk away. Without water everything in sight was extremely dirty. She immediately saw a tremendous number of needs—raw, physical needs. The level of malnutrition could be seen easiest in the children. Mama John identified in some a stage of malnutrition called kwashiorkor, characterized by a large potbelly, depigmentation of the skin, and a loss of hair. She identified others who had passed this stage and were now experiencing the most severe stage of malnutrition called marasmus, characterized by a wasting away of the body. Hungry flies surrounded infected eyes and ears as well as skin rashes such as scabies. This famine, however, affected more than just the children. Mama John saw disease present in every age group. How she longed to talk with them, to comfort them. Yet, she could not communicate in the Amharic language. Real communication would have to come from her actions.

A feeding center was established on the outskirts of Rabel in a building that originally had been built by the government as a craft center. The building was partitioned into one large area and two smaller areas. One of the smaller areas was to be Mama John's room. The second small area was for Sally Jones, a nurse who had also come as a volunteer.

Mama John's room contained a bed that had been built for her by young men who were a part of the feeding team. A thin foam pad covered the wooden slats that held her off the floor. The wood had been brought in from Addis Ababa. Mama John was often thankful for her bed because it kept her away from the cold, windy drafts and away from the rats that prowled at night.

One day a young Ethiopian team member stopped her. "We have a surprise for you tonight, Mama John," he said.

"A surprise?" she asked.

"You'll see when you go in your room."

All the team members grinned as they watched Mama John.

She knew she couldn't wait, so she went immediately to her room, and there she saw their surprise. The legs of her bed had been put into five-gallon tins that had been emptied of their contents and then filled with water. Notes were attached to each tin. Mama John began to laugh as she read the notes aloud. They stated, "RATS STAY OUT!"

She replied, "I didn't know that Ethiopian rats could read English!"

Beyond the humor, Mama John was touched that the young men had understood her dislike of rats and tried to help. She wondered if they had noticed the empty camera film canisters that she had used to block the bigger rat holes.

Her room was filling up. A small table built with wood left over from the bed now stood in the corner. The other piece of furniture in the room was her trunk which held her supply of clothes and a picture of her husband. She had been given many baskets that the women had woven. These now hung from the ceiling and walls. For now, this was home.

Water was difficult to obtain, so Mama John limited the time and water she used for cleanup. Each morning she obtained a small cup of water to brush her teeth. The window at the back of her room served as a sink from which she spit. Looking out, she could see her latrine. She bragged that she had the only two-seater in town.

Every two weeks or so Mama John washed her hair. In the morning she put a pan of water out in the sunshine to take the chill off of it, and then asked one of the guards to help her.

"Talaum, are you ready?" Mama John motioned to the man who stood guard.

"I'm coming," the tall armed guard answered.

As part of a now accepted routine, Talaum laid his machine gun against the wall of the hut in order to lift up the bucket and pour. Mama John leaned over and untied the long, thinning gray strands.

"Go slowly now, remember."

"I know how," the guard responded, grinning.

The hair washing took just a few minutes with so little water.

"Thank you," said Mama John, as she smiled and rubbed her head with a towel.

The lanky guard smiled back his response. He was happy to help this unusual woman with her unusual request.

Four women had been hired to carry water from a small mountain

Mama John holding a loving, young recipient of food and medical care.

stream three miles away. All day they carried water in clay pots on their backs from the stream to a large barrel in the building. This water was for all the needs at the feeding station. It was handled with a great deal of care and appreciation for it was a precious commodity.

One day the young men of the team killed a goat. They shared a leg with Mama John. She cooked it that day, happy that she would have meat to eat for awhile. Then she heard the helicopter bringing in supplies. Two Canadian pilots were on board. They smelled the meat and soon all three were seated around her little table prepared for a feast. None of them had eaten meat in a while, and before long, it was all gone!

Another visitor who came Mama John's way was a young English doctor. He had heard that there was an *old lady* helping to run a clinic and he wanted to see this himself. Mama John took him on a tour of the clinic. There were many who were extremely ill, but the doctor took special interest in the children. From that day on until the young doctor returned to England, the last helicopter drop of the day would always have a package in it labeled "For Mama John." In it would be pieces of hard candy for the children.

As time went by, Mama John tried to include her family in her daily life. In one letter she wrote:

*March 25, 1985*

*Dear family,*

*I'm sitting here thinking about my daddy, for the only light I have is an old lantern like the one he used to carry on the railroad so many years ago.*

*At night the stars are so very near you feel as though you could touch them. I find myself each evening saying again and again, "The heavens declare the glory of God." It really is so beautiful and the only thing beautiful my physical eyes see. So much hunger . . . such rags . . . overwhelming. And yet, I have felt such power in the presence of God.*

*We start our day at 8:00 A.M. with morning devotions with the staff. We are eight: Sally Jones, six fine Ethiopian men, and me. We are well organized so that even though we've had some problems we are usually in bed by 9:00 P.M. I do get so very tired. I guess it's more emotional tiredness even though we do work hard. Today we finally finished, I mean quit, about 6:45 P.M. When darkness comes we have no other choice. We do try to see that no one leaves without food, but the job is so big.*

*I've cried more in the last couple of weeks than I have in a lifetime. I'm sure my life is changed. This is truly a communistic state. We're monitored and watched by guards with guns. I still don't get any answers as to why. Why is this necessary among these sick and starving people?*

*I just finished my supper which was eggs and a piece of very, very dry bread that I fried to try and soften a bit.*

*Sally isn't well tonight so she's gone to bed. Please pray for me that my eyes, my voice, and my touch will be a channel of God's love. Tonight an old man came, and before I could stop him he was kissing my feet. Pray for me that all I do will portray God's love.*

*Mama John*

In the weeks to come her tears continued to fall like rain on the parched Ethiopian soil. Death was a daily reality not sought after, but accepted and expected. Perhaps the hardest part for Mama John was the children.

One day several children came to Mama John for help. They told her that their parents would not speak to them. When she arrived at their home, she could easily see why the parents could not speak. They were dead. Later the children told of how their parents had insisted on giving them all the food they could find, eating none themselves.

As more children found their way to the feeding center, they told stories of running as fast as they could for fear of the hyenas. With their young eyes they had seen what happened to those who were too weak to flee from these prowling, hungry predators. The young Ethiopian team leaders did not let Mama John outside the compound at times for the sights there were beyond description. Later they wept as they helped bury half-eaten bodies of those who had gotten so close yet not close enough to the help available.

One day the team leaders dug a hole for a young child who had died. The mother gave the naked corpse to Mama John to hold. Mama John searched around for part of a blanket to wrap the body in. As she looked down at the limp body, too young for all the suffering it had known, she began to sob. In frustration she turned her back to the small band of people and cried aloud, "God, where are you?" The wind whipped the words from her mouth. No one had even heard her cry.

Again she screamed, "God, where are you?"

Tears poured down her cheeks as she wept without control. She felt utterly alone and desolate. All that was within her screamed out in rebellion against the injustice she witnessed daily. Then John 4:24 came to mind: "God is spirit, and those who worship Him must worship in spirit and truth." Mama John knew that her worship of God was not confined to a certain place or situation. This verse reminded her that true worship is beyond mere human ability.

God's Spirit within her would enable her to understand how to worship God even with a dead child in her arms. To worship her Father must be a complete surrender to Him even in the darkest of moments and in the most difficult of places. Once again she surrendered her will to the will of God the Creator. The pain from the death of one so innocent remained, but once again Mama John knew inner peace that is found only in the presence of God.

Mama John knew what a mother's love meant. How she groaned inwardly as she saw mothers come for help only to leave with their arms empty; their babies too far gone to save. As she watched these mothers' arms swing loosely by their sides, Mama John ached for them. She could not help but think of her own children and grandchildren. She knew that they were praying for her, and she continued to write, sharing her life in pen and paper.

*March 28, 1985*

*My dear granddaughter, Rachel,*

*I think about you so much and love you more than words can say. I really feel deep in my heart that you are praying for me as I work here in Ethiopia. I really need your help. Will you help me?*

*This is my problem. We have built a big shelter for the children that are very weak because they have been hungry for so long. It has a dirt floor and each child is given a blanket. We feed them three times a day. Twice a day I give them vitamins and a very special milk mixture. Some of the bigger children are already feeling so much better. They are beginning to come outside of the shelter now and play. My problem is their having something to play with. I need something for them, some toys like a ball or a yo-yo or any small toys that Baba John could put into his suitcase. Baba John will be coming here in May and I will write him and tell him that you are going to help the children of Ethiopia in this way. I do believe that they will be happier children if they have something to play with and I am so happy that I have a granddaughter like you who I can write to when I need some help.*

*Please say hello to your family for me. I love you.*

*Mama John*

Mama John's four-year-old granddaughter, Rachel, was learning from the example set before her. After receiving the letter, she quietly went to her room and closed the door. She packed all of her clothes except two play outfits and two dresses.

"I don't really need these other clothes," she said. "The children that Mama John is helping need them more than I do. Could I please share too?"

And so her clothes were sent along with the toys that had been requested.

As relief efforts continued, more and more needs were discovered. One day a Canadian pilot spotted something moving below him as he flew his normal distribution route. He landed the chopper to explore. There he found a group of Ethiopian Orthodox priests starving to death. Flying on to Rabel, he asked Mama John to accompany him and visit these 40 men. She agreed to go with him.

They found the priests living in a cavelike structure built in the side of a mountain. They suffered from many illnesses along with malnutrition. Mama John had brought food and medicine, which she dispensed. During the visit the oldest of the group asked Mama John if she would like to see where they worshipped God. She was taken to a small clearing inside the cave. There, the sun's rays filtered through, creating intricate patterns in the dusty air. The silence was profound. Looking around she saw an erect T-shaped staff.

"What is that for?" she asked.

"This," said the priest as he touched the staff, "this is my leaning stick. Each week, from Friday to Monday I fast, I pray, and I lean upon this staff as I seek God with all my heart."

"So, you and I, in our hearts, are alike," responded Mama John.

"How can this be?" the priest asked.

"I, too, have sought God with all my heart. And, I know, in my heart, that I have found Him."

The old priest's eyes lit up. He gathered the men together and begged Mama John to tell more. Sitting with the holy men she shared about the God of Creation. Then she told of His Son, Christ Jesus, and of a book called the Bible, God's holy book.

"We have heard of this book, but it is in a language we cannot understand, a language that was used by priests of old," shared her newfound friend.

Mama John asked if any among them could read Amharic, the current language of Ethiopia. There were some who could.

"I will send this book to you," she promised as she rose to leave.

That week she arranged for the pilot to airdrop a Bible in Amharic to them.

Weeks later the priests traveled to Rabel. They came bringing gifts of water pots, teapots, and goblets fashioned with their own hands.

"We bring you gifts to thank you," their leader said.

All the priests had come, walking many miles. They wanted to thank this woman who had given them the key to the mystery in their search for the true God.

Mama John learned much from her Ethiopian brothers and sisters. They had a strength and a persistence that had to be admired. Each time there was a possibility of rain the Ethiopians went out to their fields and began to plow in preparation for the rain. It had not rained in ten years and yet they continued to prepare. With the oxen all gone they plowed with primitive handheld plows over ground that was mostly rocky soil. Yet they plowed and prepared. God had blessed this noble and gracious people with the ability to keep on hoping.

There were many difficult times too. The team in Rabel was dependent upon the food and supplies brought in by helicopter, airplane, or truck. Many nations joined together in this hunger relief venture. For food to arrive at the feeding center, a Polish team brought in a ground crew to clear the area below Rabel. This involved setting off flare guns to frighten the hungry birds away. Then they set up radio communications with an English team who had a large transport plane. After the large plane dropped the food, the Canadian

Sharing joy and hope in the midst of suffering.

helicopter pilots airlifted it a portion at a time. The Russians, Swiss, and Germans also brought in supplies from time to time.

For those living in Rabel, these supplies were their only link with the outside world. The rising canyons that surrounded them became the walls of their small world. It was a life as rugged as the countryside.

For Mama John, not knowing the language continued to be a frustration. Early one morning she read in 2 Corinthians 2:15 how Christians are to be as a pleasant aroma. She began to pray, "Lord, let me be like this sweet fragrance. Today, as I move among these people, even though I can't speak their language, let me be like a living fragrance of Your love and Your power." While she was praying, her Bible fell to the floor. Still praying, she leaned to pick it up. Then, she noticed the room began to smell; it was an awful scent. Mama John opened her eyes and realized that as she had leaned over to pick up her Bible, the candle flame had caught her hair on fire. Grabbing her blanket she quickly smothered her singeing hair. Not too much damage had been done. Laughing, she said aloud, "Lord, that wasn't quite what I had in mind for the fragrance!"

To continue living in Rabel, Mama John knew that she must be filled with a power beyond her own. Each day brought an intensity beyond belief and despair beyond endurance. Many times she became overwhelmed.

*April 12, 1985*

*Dearest family,*

*We desperately need grain and medicine. The helicopter is out this week. The road is out as well. We hope that the helicopter will start dropping supplies again on Monday. The trucks should be getting through before this. In the meantime we're just dividing out what we have.*

*I wish you could walk through, or should I say cry through, a day with me. The hours are long. I've not had one day off since I arrived five weeks ago. The work is hard and at night I'm exhausted. Yet, I love what I'm doing. Seeing God at work refreshes me even when physical tiredness is overwhelming.*

*The tears still come. Some days it seems as though I cry all day. I pray someday I'll be able to express all that I've experienced here.*

*I have only one envelope. I'm hoping that someone will be coming this way and will bring me some air forms. I really am at the end of the line. There is no communication except if we listen for the helicopter when it makes its drops, catch the pilot's attention, and ask if he can get word to Addis. No electricity, no radio, little water.*

*Your prayers are seeing me through some really difficult days. Tonight I'm quite homesick. Even so, it's going to be tough when I have to leave these people and even more so the six young Ethiopians I work with. They have really put themselves in my heart.*

*I have been writing by this kerosene lantern for about an hour and my eyes don't want to focus. I love you and miss you.*

*Mama John*

Before she left, Davis had given Mama John a small tape recorder. She had planned to record at the end of each day what her experiences had been so she could share them with him. Quickly she realized that this was too difficult, so she packed the tape recorder away.

One morning about 3:00 A.M. Mama John awoke. She thought she was dreaming, for she heard the sound of rain beating on the tin roof over her head; but the rain was real. She lit a candle and rummaged around in her trunk until she found the tape recorder. Pushing "record" she continued to listen and to praise God for sending the rain. Over and over she said, "Praise the Lord, Davis, it's raining." What a beautiful sound to her ears. Throughout the next hour she continued recording raindrop after raindrop.

Mama John tenderly holds a child at the clinic.

Weeks later Davis received the tape from his wife. It was the first he had received from her, and he looked forward to hearing the specifics of her life. He was preparing for a trip so he waited until he began to drive to listen to it so he could listen without interruption.

At first he thought something was wrong with the recording, for he could hear only static. Then he heard a voice in the background, "Praise the Lord, it's raining. Davis, praise the Lord, it's raining." He sensed her joy and worship, and the tears began to fall. Pulling off the road, Davis continued to weep as he listened to the voice of his wife so many miles away. Rain had come to Rabel!

As the rains continued to fall, Mama John put pen to paper to share her thoughts.

*June 20, 1985*

*Dearest family,*

*The rains have come and we are deeply grateful even though it's so very cold and so much mud. It comes with blessing and yet, more sickness.*

*The people are not only hungry but so very ragged. The shelter people are warm for they get blankets but the ones on the outside—how it hurts. What to do? There are so many and it seems that more and more come every day.*

*Lynn Groce and James Hampton came last night and left early this morning. Lynn wasn't too encouraging about my replacement anytime soon. It's the government on this side that is holding things up. Sally leaves in a couple of weeks. She is ready to go. This is a tough assignment for one so young.*

*Yesterday and today the Germans and the Royal Air Force of England have been making airdrops of grain. They have to drop the food in the valley below because we are 10,000 feet up on the edge of the canyon. Then a helicopter uses a sling to bring the grain to our camp.*

*The truck came into our camp today with seed. Tomorrow we're expecting hundreds of farmers to come for seed. I like this time.*

*Soon we're to open another feeding center at Merhabete. There are thousands starving there and no one has reached them yet. This means our team breaks up. So sad, but necessary. We'll get another three young men and send three of ours to help in the new area. Pray that the government will give us permits for nurses to come in.*

*Our helicopter was taking Harry Belafonte back to Addis this week. He dropped down for a visit with us. He's out for the US artists for Africa.*

*Yameni, my precious young man who helps in the clinic, built me a headboard for my bed today. I wish you could see it. I'm so proud of it. He knows I go to bed early to read and get warm. He says I can read better now. I can. My candle is flickering so I'll close.*

*I love you. God is so good.*

*Mama John*

As the time approached for Mama John to leave Rabel, she felt many mixed emotions. The tumult inside spilled out in tears at a moment's notice. Her life there had been an exercise of moment by moment dependence upon her Creator. It was He Who had given her a love for the Ethiopian people. She had become caught up in their very existence. Could she leave these whom she had come to love above life itself?

Hard work and minimal eating had taken their toll on Mama John's body. Her hair, always so thick, was falling out in handfuls now. She did not need to look in a mirror or get on scales to know that she was 40 pounds lighter. Her pants were held up by suspenders given to her by Ed Mason.

She struggled with a decision to leave. There was no nurse to replace her. Her assignment of four months had now stretched into five. For four weeks she had received a message from Davis each time the helicopter had dropped its load. It was always the same. "Mary, come home. Davis." But how could she leave? Finally Ed Mason came to visit her.

"Mary," he said. "Davis is my boss and he is saying that you need to come home."

"You're right, Ed," she replied, "Davis is the boss and you tell him that as soon as he sends a nurse to replace me, I'll come home."

Finally news arrived that a nurse was on her way, complete with the required governmental permission. Early one morning Mama

1989, Ethiopia: A warm welcome for the returning Mama John!

John asked God to give her a peace about her departure. Putting on her glasses, she adjusted her eyes to the flickering candlelight, turned to her New Testament, and began to read. The assurance she needed came from John 17:4 in a conversation between the Father and His Son. Jesus said to His Father, "I glorified Thee on the earth, having accomplished the work which Thou hast given Me to do."

In that moment she knew that although the needs in Rabel were still overwhelming, she had done the part that the Father had given her to do. There were other opportunities ahead, and she must go forward to meet them. That same week, with tears flowing freely, she bid farewell to those who had come to mean so much to her in Rabel.

For the next four years, as she was needed, Mama John returned again and again to Ethiopia to help in relief nursing. On her first return to Rabel hundreds came to meet the plane. As it

1995: Mary returns to a friend's victory garden in Charleston, South Carolina.

landed, Mama John was lifted from the doorway and held high in the air by many loving hands. She saw the faces of the young Ethiopian men with whom she had shared both laughter and tears. She saw the faces of the many children with their mothers. With joy they welcomed her back and carried her in their arms. Looking around, she saw that she was surrounded by those whom she had cared for. They called out, "Mama John! Mama John!"

Throughout her life, Mama John has been loving and caring for people: in Mogadishu, Rabel, Richmond, Mathari Valley, Arusha, Shauri Moya, Igede, and Charleston. Her name has been called by many. She has given the touch of Christ's love through her healing hands and compassionate heart. To Him is due all honor and glory.